# Succeed With Senior Clients:
## A Financial Advisor's Guide To Best Practices

CAROLYN L. ROSENBLATT, R.N., ATTORNEY AT LAW
DR. MIKOL DAVIS, GERONTOLOGIST, PSYCHOLOGIST

*all the best,*
*Carolyn Rosenblatt*

Copyright © 2016 AgingInvestor.com
All rights reserved.
ISBN 978-0-692-70250-5
Library of Congress Control Number: 2016908223

Cover design by Charles Brucaliere
Editing by Deborah Markson-Katz

No part of this book may be reproduced, transmitted in any form or by any means, mechanical or electronic, including photocopying or recording, or by any information storage and retrieval system, without the express written permission of the authors, except for the use of brief quotations in a book review. For permission contact AgingInvestor.com.

**PUBLISHER'S NOTE:**
The purpose of this book is to provide information and to educate. Neither author intends that the information contained herein is to be construed as personal legal, health, psychological or medical advice. If personal medical, legal or other expert assistance or consultation is required by any reader, the services of a competent professional should be sought. The authors make no representations or warranties with respect to the accuracy or completeness of the contents of this work and specifically disclaim any liability, loss or risk that is incurred as a consequence of the use and application of the contents of this book.

Ordering Information: Bulk discounts are available on quantity purchases by financial services corporations, associations and others. Customized versions of this book are also available for bulk purchasers. Special consideration is given to professional organizations. For details, contact AgingInvestor.com.

**DEDICATION**

To our grandmothers, Louise Blondeau Crum (Carolyn) and Elizabeth Davis (Mikol), who taught us how to age with grace. Both were inspirations in our lives.

# CONTENTS

**Preface** *ix*
**Introduction** *xii*

## Chapter 1
## Know the Aging Clients' Red Flags                1

*Aging As a Concern for Financial Services Professionals*
*What You Need to Know About Alzheimer's Disease*
*What the Regulators Want You to Do About Aging Clients*
*The Red Flags for Diminished Capacity*
*Your Observations and Their Importance*

## Chapter 2
## Nuts and Bolts:
## What Are the Components of Financial Capacity?   26

*Common Yet Dangerous Assumptions*
*Creating Your Own Checklist for Documenting Capacity Issues*
*Do Clients Have a Right to Do What They Want With Their Own Money?*
*Definition of the Specifics of Financial Capacity—The Nine Areas*
*Measuring Financial Capacity With Testing*
    *Resistance*
    *Using Fiduciaries*
    *Client Retention*
    *Escalation*

## Chapter 3
## Financial Elder Abuse:
## How You Can Fight the Crime of the Century       52

*How Big Is the Elder Abuse Problem and Why Is This Important?*
*Who Is Stealing From Your Aging Clients?*
*A Common Kind of Abuse—The Family Member and Undue Influence*
*What Can the Advisor Do?*
*Should You Report Financial Elder Abuse?*
*The Warning Signs*
*Caregiver Abuse*
*Telephone Scams, Internet Thieves and "Front Door Fraud"*
*Professional Financial Abuse*
*The Solution*

## Chapter 4
### Tough Talk: Communication Challenges With Aging Clients  76
*What's Different About Older Clients?*
*Secrecy About Finances*
*How Secrecy Can Cause You to Lose Clients*
*A Solution: The Power of Your Relationship*
*The Risk of Waiting Too Long*
*Why Is This Your Problem and Not Just the Family's?*
*Other Communication Issues With Aging Memory Loss —*
  *What You Should Do and Say to Your Client*
*Physical Impairments as Communication Challenges—*
  *Hearing Loss, Pace, Accessibility, Visual Impairment*
*Our Ageist Society*
*Solutions*
*What You Can Do About Resistance*

## Chapter 5
### Your Client's Family: An Open Book or Pandora's Box?  97
*Should You Involve Your Client's Family in His Financial Affairs?*
*What Family Business Succession Planning Misses With Aging Clients*
*The Gap in Estate Planning*
*The Elements of a Successful Family Meeting*
*What to Do With Difficult Clients, Difficult Family*
*Can You Get Paid for Doing This?*
*What Is Family Mediation?*
*The Privacy Issue in Families*
*The Long-Term Care Issue*

## Chapter 6
### Preemptive Strike:
### Hit the Aging Client Problem Before It Hits You  123
*The Beginning: Segregating Senior Investors and Greater*
  *Frequency of Communication*
*The Emergency Contact Person*
*Training Firm Employees on Senior-Specific Issues*
*Areas of Concern for Regulators and Essential Steps for Compliance*
*The Successor Trustee on the Family Trust*
*Compliance Officers*

## Chapter 7
## The Elephant in the Room:
## Advisors Themselves With Diminished Capacity   141
*The Problem No One Talks About*
*Illustration: The Financial Advisor With Dementia*
*Do You Know the Signs?*
*Ethical Considerations*
*Things We Can Borrow From the Legal Profession*
*Possible Solutions*
*One Simple Thing Every Independent Advisor Should Do*

## Chapter 8
## Wrap-Up: Take Action Today   166
*Policy-Driven Actions*
*A One-Step-at-a-Time Approach*
*The Best Outcomes*
*Should You Wait?*
*The Measure of True Learning*

## About the Authors   177

**Appendix 1:** *Checklist: 10 Warning Signs of Diminished Capacity*   179
**Appendix 2:** *Checklist: 7 Warning Signs of Financial Elder Abuse*   180
**Appendix 3:** *Busy Advisors' Quick Start Senior Program Checklist*   182
**Appendix 4:** *Resources and Helpful Internet Links*   184

## AgingInvestor.com Social Media Channels   188

# PREFACE

A personal evolution was the impetus for this book. Dr. Davis and I had been working with the families of aging parents for a few years when our own financial advisor suggested that we speak to a group of advisors about aging and wealth transfers. We did our presentation on why it is so difficult for wealthy and powerful aging patriarchs and matriarchs to give up the reins of financial control. We talked about secrecy over finances and why people in families have trouble disclosing information their family members need.

We talked about aging itself, the powerful forces and fears that drive holding on to control over finances, sometimes until the person in charge is dangerously impaired. We talked about how losses result. We talked about what advisors could DO about this. And when we finished, a flood of questions came from our audience. All of them were experienced advisors, wealth managers and broker-dealers. None of them seemed to have any more than a very rudimentary awareness of the aging process and how it impacts finances, decisions about money and family wealth transfers. We responded to these very legitimate questions until time ran out. And email questions followed. We could see a need.

Afterward, we had a number of talks together reflecting on the experience. It was husband-and-wife talk about family. It was professional partners' talk about our consulting business. We felt dismay that millions of Baby Boomers are reaching retirement age, and living longer than ever after that. And we worried. If the folks managing assets for all these millions did not clearly understand the particular risks of aging in their clients, how could they address the real problems of their oldest clients effectively?

## SUCCEED WITH SENIOR CLIENTS

We were quite happy advising families about their aging loved ones and helping them resolve family conflicts at AgingParents.com. We had started this advice and conflict resolution business in 2007. But because of the speaking experiences, we saw beyond families to the entire financial services field. Other than our presentations, we had not offered them a thing, and they had the same issues to face, from a different perspective, that families also face. They all questioned what to do about age-related problems and how they impact money decisions and management. And here we were, aging experts with three professions between us, over 90 years of combined experience relevant to what we were seeing, and we were not addressing it with financial professionals but for the periodic public speaking engagements.

We asked financial advisors if they thought there was a need in their industry for information or education about aging clients. Consistently the answer was "yes." People wanted quick answers to complex issues, which is perhaps human nature. But there are no quick answers. We began researching what financial advisors could get from their own industry sources. The result: not much. The quality was superficial, and the quantity of things like continuing education was sparse. The focus of any course material we found was about how to plan for retirement and how to make assets last. It rarely dealt with cognitive impairment, one of aging's major risks. And no wonder. The material came from the industry itself, not from outside the industry, where aging expertise would be a logical source for the needed data.

Thus began our evolution, from working only with families and elders themselves, to working with the financial services industry. We created a new outlet, AgingInvestor.com. We began to read all manner of industry publications on how professionals were dealing with aging clients. We could see that our skills could be useful. Writing to a different audience began.

Over and over we heard, "Do you have anything on best practices? Do you have anything we can use as a quick reference? Do you have anything that I can use to become more skilled without having to become an expert myself? We're really busy." And we set to work.

This book resulted from answering questions financial professionals asked us. It came from listening to what seemed to be bothering the financial advisor, wealth manager, broker or other with an impaired older client. It is also a result of working to crystalize the most important pieces of helpful information about aging clients we could assemble and making them user-friendly for your industry.

No one in financial services has to be an aging expert, but if you have even one aging client, you need to know what to do if your client demonstrates cognitive decline. You want to excel at your job. Acquiring knowledge about how to successfully manage the older client is one way to reach a new level of excellence.

We say this book is about best practices. We've worked to make our descriptions of best practices easy to understand and practical.

These are ideals. Any one of the things we mention can be used with any client who presents with an issue that is age-related. There are no mandates yet that will force this on you, though you can expect some in the future. But even without mandates, the best professionals will strive for a skill set that applies to the broad category of clients living into their 80s, 90s and beyond. May you be one of those excellent professionals. And we sincerely hope that this book will help guide you along your way.

Carolyn Rosenblatt and Dr. Mikol Davis

## INTRODUCTION

Why should you have to worry about aging clients? What's the big deal? They're not investing new money, they're taking it out. Don't you have enough to do already, with trying to protect their assets and following all the industry's rules? You're probably thinking, I'm doing fine right now. Don't give me any more tasks! As long as I'm protecting portfolios against loss, I should be thanked, not given more responsibilities.

But consider this: Not adding more responsibilities would be fine if people didn't grow older and start to lose clarity of judgment, wouldn't it? And it would be fine if the regulators weren't breathing down your neck, ready to push a lot of elder-related mandates on you.

If aging clients would just stay competent to the end of life we'd all be fine. It would be great if no one developed dementia or lost the ability to make financial decisions. But the truth is, our population is aging, and we'll soon be seeing more walkers and wheelchairs on the streets than baby strollers. Given that, every financial professional automatically has been handed more responsibility. It is unavoidable. When you have aging clients, the risk is constant that some will become too incapacitated to make sound financial decisions. It's not a rare occurrence but a statistical reality. And if you aren't paying close attention, they will get ripped off and you will lose fees. Financial abuse causes *your* clients and everyone else's to lose more than $36 billion a year. Your income drains away when money is taken from your clients by fraud and theft.

Preventing their losses and, consequently, your loss of fees is a treacherous maze when your client has diminished capacity. And statistics show us that **the average advisor has seven cli-**

**ents right now with diminished capacity.** If you think they are safe because you go over their portfolios with them every year, or that they're far too experienced, sophisticated or intelligent to do something stupid with their money, think again. Pick just one of your wealthy clients who is age 75 or older right now. Imagine that you lose that client next week for reasons we discuss in this book. They get rid of you or you get rid of them. Calculate the loss of fees for that person's assets under management if she lives to be 90. It's not unusual to live to be 90 years of age these days. And you may have seven or more of those aging folks as clients. Do the math. Are you getting the picture? Your aging clients are sitting ducks. Age alone makes them vulnerable. In this book we explain just how that happens and what you need to do about it.

I'm Carolyn Rosenblatt, an R.N. and elder law attorney. My co-author is Dr. Mikol Davis, a clinical psychologist focused on aging individuals. We are a husband-and-wife team dedicated to preventing financial abuse of the aging folks among us. We wrote this book specifically for financial services professionals with busy lives who don't have the time to study a lot of aging information while working at their regular jobs. We have decades of experience in working with families who have aging loved ones. We spend much of our time consulting with families and professionals who are struggling with things that fall within a grey area: the question of competency of the aging person. And we're in the situation ourselves, with Mikol's 93-year-old mom still alert and making financial decisions.

Most professionals outside the health care arena do not have any specific training regarding aging and, as a result, are largely unprepared for managing a client with age-related difficulty. Even if an aging parent or grandparent in your own life had dementia, or became frail as he aged, that does not prepare you for your clients and their unique challenges surrounding their finances. This book will give you some shortcuts to better expertise.

It will also offer **an overall plan to help you stop losing money because your aging clients are being taken advantage of by others**. You are in an excellent position to take action to stop these losses. You'll learn what to watch for, and knowing those red flags will bring you greater confidence. You'll learn how to be proactive rather than reactive, as most financial advisors are now. You wait until you see a problem and then try to figure out how to solve it. Sometimes that leaves you with no good choices. You can lose the client because there was no plan in mind.

You may be forced to get rid of a client because you did not involve a third party when diminished capacity first reared its head. Or you may wait too long to act, and then a crisis causes you to escalate the matter, but no one has a solution this late in the game. Compliance then tells you to get rid of the client; too much liability risk. We want to help you avoid that situation.

Our purpose is also to enable you to honor your older clients, to treat them with the dignity they deserve and to show them that you do more than just manage money. Knowing how to take protective action will help prevent loss. You are in a unique position to do that: You can really get to know your clients.

Think about this: Many clients' families are scattered across the country and around the world. Some families have a lot of communication problems. You, having regular contact with a client at least yearly, if not more often, are in a special position of trust and knowledge. You probably spend more time with your client than her doctor, who is likely limited to a brief visit and a quick look at a medical problem. Even the client's physician is limited in how well she knows your client and what is going on in her life. Adult children and grandchildren may or may not have regular contact and may not know anything about your client's financial picture. You may be the only one, or one of the only ones, in her life who understands her finances, her preferences about spending and her long-term resources. You also know how much your client depends on advice. She can get very bad advice and be persuaded to do disastrous things if no one is watching. That's precisely how assets get drained away by predators. And clients get easily pulled in by a persuasive pitch from "such a nice person," who is a wolf in sheep's clothing.

These predatory people are out there, and they're everywhere. They can be family members, the next-door neighbor, a caregiver or any professional. They devise clever ways to get your client to give them money, sometimes millions of dollars, over time. This is why we want you to keep watch. Learn how to spot the vulnerabilities in your aging clients. Take action. And we suggest what action will be most effective.

Our motivation is to help you assist your aging client in better ways than ever before. Our aim is to guide you in expanding your role as an advisor who has special expertise with our older investors. We help you see new ways of setting them on an organized and well-thought-out path. You don't want to lose clients when you see, or even sense, that trouble is brewing because of age-related issues. If you ignore this, it is a sure thing you will lose clients unnecessarily.

**PROTECTING YOURSELF**

When you manage aging clients wisely you are protecting yourself as well as the vulnerable person whose portfolio you manage. If anything in this book helps you avoid prosecution, or being questioned for not acting reasonably regarding these elders, we will be meeting our goals in writing.

We will also be meeting our goals if you follow our prevention suggestions about how to avoid losing impaired clients. We explain how this is done by making use of opportunities to bring trusted third parties into the picture while correctly addressing the privacy issue. And if your actions stop even a single case of financial elder abuse, that would be an excellent outcome as well.

## OUR STORY

We, as authors, share a common love for aging folks, probably arising in both cases from close and loving relationships with our respective grandmothers.

We were inspired by them, and we were both taught the value of honoring those who become vulnerable because of age and the subsequent toll it takes on mind and body.

For Carolyn, with both a nursing career and a long career in litigation representing injured individuals, there is a passion for justice and for the highest ethics with clients. For Mikol, more than 44 years of being a provider of mental health services was always motivated by compassion for those who need help. Together, we offer our combined expertise in aging issues to broaden what you have already learned about any aging client.

Throughout the book we offer you illustrations of the issues with real case studies. We can all learn from others and how their actions did or did not help. We hope the things that turned out well will inspire you and the ones that didn't go well will motivate you.

# 1
# KNOW THE AGING CLIENTS' RED FLAGS

**INTRODUCTION**

In this chapter, we consider how much of an aging client issue we are really facing right now. We look at the impact of aging on financial decision-making, understanding that age is a risk factor for dementia. We briefly go through dementia and Alzheimer's disease, then discuss how these are often age-related.

Most advisors want to know what they should look for in aging clients so they can tell if a person has diminished capacity. You don't want information overload. We're making it simple here. We show you the red flags and explain how to decide if a person really does have diminished capacity or whether there is some other reasonable explanation for the client's behavior that you are observing.

**How Big a Concern Is Aging for Financial Services Professionals?**

It's big. By the year 2020 nearly one in every six Americans will be 65 or older.[1] If you were thinking that perhaps you could wait to deal with these issues, please reconsider. We are facing a wave of older people in our population, and not only is the number growing but people are living longer than ever before. In

---

[1] U.S. Census Bureau projections:
http://www.census.gov/population/www/projections/files/nation/summary/np2008-t2.xls.

2015 our government honored the oldest WWII veterans. One was 110 years of age! Another was 105 years old. And these are only a few of some publicly acknowledged examples.

Most of us know someone in his 90s, or perhaps a centenarian or two. Mikol's mother is 93 as of this writing, and she has investments as well as opinions about them. This is an example of what we are now facing as professionals with the generation of parents of Baby Boomers. And then there are the Boomers themselves, a population of some 73 million. Leading-edge Boomers, those born in 1946, are now turning, or are already, 70 as of this writing.

If you're thinking, "So what?" think about this: The risk of diminished capacity is age-related. The occurrence of dementia, a symptom of Alzheimer's disease, and other forms of dementia rises with age. What that means for you is that any client who is a senior, defined by our government as being 65 or older, is at some risk for dementia. And no one with dementia should be permitted to make complex financial decisions as the symptoms of this disease increase. Your clients are simply not safe any longer to judge risk and process the information you give them. Worse yet, they are an easy mark for any ruthless person who wants to use your client's diminished capacity as an easy way to manipulate them—in the form of signing over checks and property, for example—giving thieves the power to take advantage of them for financial gain. And it's a lot easier for a predator to do this than rob a bank. Sadly, most elder abuse is never reported to authorities.

Given that diminished capacity is often a result of Alzheimer's disease or other dementia, we examine what that is and what is meant by dementia.

## SUCCEED WITH SENIOR CLIENTS

**What You Need to Know About Alzheimer's Disease**
Alzheimer's is a disease that causes the progressive death of nerve cells in the brain. The person with Alzheimer's loses the ability to think clearly and, in particular, to assess financial risks. The disease eventually destroys one's ability to safely make judgments about investments. There is no cure and not yet a proven effective treatment that will even slow it down. It can last from 8 to 20 years. The onset is usually very subtle.[2]

**The greatest known risk factor for Alzheimer's is advancing age.** Most individuals with the disease are 65 or older. The likelihood of developing Alzheimer's doubles about every five years after age 65. After age 85 the risk rises. One in three people age 85 and up are diagnosed with Alzheimer's disease. Some statistics report the risk at that age being nearly 50%. One of the greatest mysteries of Alzheimer's is why risk rises so dramatically as we grow older.[3] About two-thirds of those affected by Alzheimer's disease are women.

**What You Need to Know About Dementia**
Dementia is a general term for a decline in mental ability severe enough to interfere with daily life.[4] Doctors often use the term "Alzheimer's" and "dementia" interchangeably. Some people think that if a person "only" has dementia, there is nothing to worry about, as "it's not Alzheimer's disease." This is not true. Dementia is considered to be a sign of Alzheimer's or a symptom of the disease, and it may be synonymous with it as well. There are numerous other types of dementias connected to dis-

---

[2] Patricia Callone, Connie Kudllacek, Barbara Vasiloff, Janaan Manternach, Roger Brumback, *A Caregiver's Guide to Alzheimer's Disease: 300 Tips For Making Life Easier*, Demos Medical Publishing, New York, NY 2006.

[3] http://www.alz.org/alzheimers_disease_causes_risk_factors.asp. (last accessed 7.27.15)

[4] http://www.alz.org/what-is-dementia.asp. (last accessed 7.27.15)

ease processes, though Alzheimer's is by far the most common.

Dementia, to put it simply, destroys a person's ability to reason, to see dangers, to measure the wisdom of what one is doing and to remember things, particularly short term. Because it is subtle but deadly, those around an elder developing this disease may not realize how vulnerable the affected person is. It does not hit the person with the disease suddenly or like that of any other disease. It is nearly invisible at first. The signs may appear sporadically, inconsistently and unpredictably. And it affects individuals differently in every case, though all dementias have some features in common. One of these is that the first sign may be short-term memory loss. At first that may not interfere with daily life, but ultimately it always will.

And it is important to understand that dementia, whether a symptom of Alzheimer's or any other type of disease like it, is ultimately fatal.

## What Do Advisors Need to Know About Dementia and Alzheimer's Disease?

Every advisor needs to understand clearly that a client who appears to have symptoms of the disease, such as memory loss and decline in mental ability that interferes with daily life, is a client who must stop making financial decisions sooner rather than later.

Studies have demonstrated that financial capacity is already significantly impaired in persons with *mild* Alzheimer's disease, and in the moderate stage of the disease all financial capacity domains are *severely impaired*.[5]

---

[5] Marson DC, Sawrie SM, Snyder S, et al. *Assessing Financial Capacity in Patients With Alzheimer's Disease: A Conceptual Model and Prototype Instrument.* Arch Neurol. 2000;57(6):877-884. (last accessed 5.1.16)

## Illustration: Leonard's Moderate Dementia and the Loss of His Assets

Leonard was a successful business owner, accumulating several million dollars in his investment portfolio over his work life. At age 72 he began to have difficulty with his short-term memory. He kept working, but this became increasingly difficult. Leonard was a single man with no children. His sister was the only person who paid close attention to his life. She grew increasingly alarmed as she realized that Leonard was not functioning well any longer. What she did not yet realize was that Leonard had started giving away money to every charity or organization that asked. Once a person starts to give to these causes, his name is sold and shared with other charities and nonprofits. Soon he had stacks of requests for donations on his desk. He gave to every one of them, larger and larger amounts.

After two years of warning signs of memory problems, his sister finally persuaded him to retire from his business. He did so and moved across the country to be nearer to her. She got a power of attorney from him and was able to see his account statements. She had known that he was giving away money, but she had no idea of the extent of his extravagant giving. She was shocked. Her once wealthy brother had less than a million dollars left! And he needed assisted living in a memory care unit, which cost thousands of dollars each month. She understood that if he used up what he had left, she and her husband might have to support him later in life.

What happened to Leonard's financial advisor over the period of time that this client was dramatically increasing his charitable giving? We'll never know, as Leonard doesn't remember.

**The question for every advisor is this: If you have an aging client who is showing signs of mental decline, should you get involved?** We say definitely yes! The reason is that you will lose assets under management if your client does what Leonard did. Leonard was still working. He was able to carry on a nice conversation, but he had no judgment left as to what was appropriate charitable giving and what was putting his own financial security at risk. The financial advisor who helped him grow his wealth certainly must have seen what was happening to the portfolio as Leonard was draining it. Should he have had the sister's contact information in his file? Should he have contacted her at the first clear signs of alarm, the red flags? Provided the advisor had permission from Leonard to contact his sister, we believe the decimation of Leonard's portfolio may have been prevented. Getting permission is a topic we do address in this book. Keep in mind that early intervention into a client's red flag behavior can allow you to keep the funds in a client's portfolio, **keep your fees coming in** and stop your client from wiping out his own security.

A client who is showing you some of the red flags may be a client who should *not* be asked to approve a financial transaction. It should be a client who has help with financial decisions. You may need to stop the client from his own financial mistakes by taking protective action.

## Suggesting Investments to Impaired Elders

It is also dangerous to ask any impaired client to assess or appreciate the risks of a new investment or change in investment patterns. It is even more dangerous when one considers how vulnerable to abuse that client can be. Getting their consent to anything is a risk to you if you have a good idea that they can't understand what you are asking of them.

The specific red flags to look for with any older adult are discussed below. However, the symptoms described do not mean that you just document them and do nothing else "until something happens." Something is already happening with a person who shows these red flags.

**The most important thing to know about Alzheimer's and dementias of any kind is that they will cause diminished capacity for financial decisions and that they will do it early in the process of development of the disease!**

Why is this so important? It is essential to understand, because your client who has these problems is going to need your help and likely will need some intervention on your part. He may ask for it. He may not. A family member may approach you asking to help an aging client with Alzheimer's disease, to avoid doing dangerous things with his investments. Will you be prepared to help that client at the request of a family member?

As a trusted advisor, you will not be able to continue to do business as usual with an impaired client. At some point you may want to contact a third party but hold back because of privacy rules. Or you may escalate the issue only to have compliance advise you to get rid of the client with cognitive impairment. But ending your relationship with the client is not the only way to address the problem. We want you to understand the alternatives so you can retain your client, with their reliable third party making financial decisions for them.

Brain disease does not necessarily jump out at you, as an advisor, unless your client is in an advanced stage. Typically the brain changes with Alzheimer's and other forms of dementia come on slowly, showing only the most subtle signs at first. Scientists believe that it could take decades to fully develop, with gradually worsening signs and symptoms that may be apparent only to those closest to the elder. The actual cause is the subject of research all over the world, but at this time it is not clearly known. Nor do we know any way to stop the progression of these brain diseases. Because of its subtlety and the hidden risks, no professional in the elder's life may be aware of the onset of Alzheimer's until the person is substantially impaired in his judgment regarding finances. In short, you have to be watching for subtle changes in your client when you first notice the warning sign of short-term memory loss, which we discuss below.

A great frustration with these brain diseases we collectively call dementia is that the person who has it may not even realize that she is impaired. A common problem is what physicians call *anosognosia*, which refers to brain-cell changes that lead to a lack of self-awareness.[6] For instance, a client could have serious memory loss and be completely unaware that he has any problem with memory at all. A simple way of looking at it is to say that the very part of the brain that would allow the client to perceive his deficits is impaired, and he simply can't recognize the deficits. This is different from denying that a problem exists. A person with anosognosia really doesn't know that he has a defect, illness or disorder. When this client tells you that things are absolutely fine in his life—even when they're obviously not—he truly believes that they are just fine.

All of our older clients are potentially vulnerable to manipulation because of brain changes. The essential concept you need to understand is that dementia is going to rob many clients of the ability to make safe financial decisions early on in the disease process *before* the client has trouble speaking or finding his way to your office. So what is the ordinary advisor, who is not an expert in psychology or medicine or the law, supposed to do with aging clients who are at risk just because of aging?

Are you required to do anything different from the way you handle older clients now?

---

[6] http://alzonline.phhp.ufl.edu/en/reading/Anosognosia.pdf. (last accessed March 12, 2015)

## What Do the Regulators Want You to Do About Aging Clients?

The regulators want you to be more protective and more alert to changes in your aging clients. They want you to have special policies so that you have a plan for taking action when the red flags go up.

In 2008 a 22-page document[7] was published by the Securities and Exchange Commission, North American Securities Administrators Association and Financial Industry Regulatory Authority, telling you what they expect you to do. None of this is yet mandatory as we write this book, but their urgings will likely become mandates in some form sooner rather than later. Model rules that you can expect will be adopted after public comments were already posted by NASAA for public view. So far those pertain to reporting of elder abuse. However, the entirety of the regulators' mission to require that advisors do specific things to keep aging clients safer is likely to emerge as model rules and then as mandates.

**To pull from that 2008 document the most important concept, we can say the regulators strongly urge that you get educated about aging clients and that you devise special policies to protect them from abuse.**

But if you're not an expert in aging or cognitive impairment, how are you supposed to know what to look for?

The problem of cognitive impairment is complex, and no one expects you to have the same expertise as a doctor or other professional trained in the field of aging. However, anyone can learn some basics, and this provides a breakdown of those basics every financial professional should know.

---

[7] *Protecting Senior Investors: Compliance, Supervisory and Other Practices Used By Financial Services Firms in Serving Senior Investors,* Securities and Exchange Commission's Office of Compliance Inspections and Examinations, North American Securities Administrators Association, and Financial Industry Regulatory Authority September 22, 2008.

## SUCCEED WITH SENIOR CLIENTS

**The Red Flags for Diminished Capacity**

Every advisor needs an understanding of the red flags indicating diminished capacity. Once you understand them, you will need a standardized way to record and track them. Comparing your observations over time will be useful, particularly at the early stages of decline, when it is harder to tell if a person is impaired or not.

After you understand, track, record them and compare them to other records you have created over time, you are ready to take the next step to protect your aging client. Your choices of those next steps will be addressed in Chapter 6 in this book. But for now let's look at a breakdown of the red flags themselves, which we divide into four categories. We take these from a work created by cooperation between the American Bar Association, the largest volunteer legal organization in the U.S., and the American Psychological Association. It is *Assessment of Older Adults With Diminished Capacity: A Handbook for Lawyers*.[8] There is a reciprocal book for psychologists. As your authors have each practiced for many years in law and psychology, respectively, we are taking the essential concepts advisors need to know from this important book and interpreting them in a way that we hope makes sense for you, as a financial professional. Your duties and obligations are different from those of lawyers and psychologists, so we have simplified the ideas to make them both understandable and practical for you to use.

You can benefit with a concise explanation from the kind of analysis lawyers and psychologists use with diminished capacity assessments. All you have to do is understand the basics and to use them as a rationale for taking further action that your in-

---

[8] *Assessment of Older Adults With Diminished Capacity: A Handbook for Lawyers*, American Bar Association and American Psychological Association, 2005, 14-16.

dustry regulators strongly suggest you take: steps to keep your client financially safe.

The following are signs you can look for in a client who is in your office. They are also things you can determine from a telephone call with a client. Watch for them. Every one is what we consider a red flag that requires your attention. If you see a few of them consistently, you will need to take swift action.

## COGNITIVE SIGNS
### 1. Memory loss
This is one of the first things most advisors may notice in a client. Perhaps she does not remember important meetings, decisions and discussions. Here are some examples of what you may see.

*Multiple telephone calls* in one day that are repetitive and do not make sense. The client forgets that she has already spoken with you and is calling about the same thing in yet another call. She repeats a question she already asked you and that you already answered.

*Client forgets why he has an appointment with you.* This can be by telephone or in person. Perhaps the client himself asked for the meeting, but then he forgets why. Or perhaps you wanted to discuss a proposed transaction with him and informed him of that, but when you call or he comes into your office, he has no idea why he is there. Trying to refresh his memory about it does not help.

*Complete forgetting of an event that just took place.* You just spent a hour with your client telling her some important information about upcoming changes to her portfolio. She seemed to understand when you were talking, but an hour later she asks you questions as if the meeting had never taken place. She had totally forgotten about it.

## SUCCEED WITH SENIOR CLIENTS

*No-shows*
You have arranged meetings, appointments with others or events that require your client's participation. He agrees on the prearranged date and time but then does not show up. When you call him, he has no recollection of the event, that others are involved or that he had agreed to this.

All of these signs are indications of short-term memory loss, which is an important early sign of developing cognitive impairment or development of dementia. There is a clear distinction between short-term memory loss, as described in the four examples above, and long-term memory.

A person may be able to clearly recall something that happened 50 years ago, as if it were yesterday. That longer-term memory does not get damaged by dementia in the same way, or at the same time, as short-term memory becomes impaired. Short-term memory loss that disrupts daily life is typically a first and early warning sign of Alzheimer's disease.[9] Do not be fooled into thinking that a client is fine because she can give you the intricate details of a place where she grew up or the work she did in her early life. That clear ability to recall things from long ago does not mean she is fine and has no cognitive impairment.

### 2. Comprehension Difficulty

Hearing a conversation or an idea is one thing, but being able to understand it is another. Comprehension difficulty may first surface when you are trying to explain a simple concept to a client and she simply doesn't get it. For instance, you might encourage your client to take some profits from an asset because of her increased cash flow needs. You tell her you want to sell XYZ. She does not appear to understand this. You go over it again. Still no sign that she gets it. This is a red flag for you.

---

[9] http://www.alz.org/alzheimers_disease_10_signs_of_alzheimers.asp.#signs.

Yes, it is also true that a lot of clients are not going to grasp basic concepts of investing. When you explain a product, their eyes glaze over and they say to just tell them what to do. That may be a normal way people deal with being overwhelmed with information that is unfamiliar. But distinguish that common situation from explaining something so simple a high school student could grasp the concept. If your client can't process simply put information, that client may be in trouble cognitively.

## 3. Communication Problems

Perhaps your client has trouble finding words he wants to express. An example would be when you want to review his account statement and he can't come up with the word "statement." He may have easily been able to do this in the past. Now he might say "that paper with the numbers," or some other roundabout description of something you commonly discuss.

Vague and disorganized language, inability to describe anything accurately and the inability to track what is going on in a conversation with you are all signs of communication difficulty. If you ask a client with communication difficulty a direct question, such as, "Have you decided what you want to do with my suggestion about selling XYZ this week?" he is unable to respond. He changes the subject, gives you an answer that doesn't address your question, or he gets lost in his own sentences and repeatedly loses his train of thought.

## 4. Lack of Mental Flexibility

Haven't we all had stubborn clients? They seem inflexible to us. Perhaps they won't listen to good advice. Perhaps they disagree, and it ends up costing them. The difference between a stubborn client and one who suffers from mental inflexibility is that the stubborn client has the ability to understand that there are other points of view beyond his own; he just chooses to ignore them. A client who has lack of mental flexibility cannot acknowledge other alternatives besides his own. He is unable to adjust to any change.

**Illustration:**
"Lydia" came into my office with her daughter, "Sarah," to meet with me for a discussion about plans for finding an alternative place to live. She had some assets left, but they were limited. She wanted to give all her money away "so the state will just take care of me from now on," she said. Her daughter had tried in vain to convince Lydia that she needed to conserve her money, live modestly and make her assets last as long as possible. She told Lydia that the state would not take care of her except in a nursing home, and Lydia was certain she did not want to go to a nursing home.

I reiterated Sarah's message and told her about the law, Medicaid and a few other basics. Lydia listened, nodded and appeared to take it all in. After a time she said she wanted to give all her money away so the state would take care of her from now on. I asked Sarah outside Lydia's presence if her mother had been told she had dementia or if she had been diagnosed. The answer was yes. Lydia is a good illustration of being unable to adjust to a needed change (find less expensive housing) to accept an alternative point of view (the state is not going to take care of you) and to accept Sarah's point of view (you need to conserve your assets).

If you have a client who demonstrates inflexibility of thinking, remember that no amount of explaining or repeating or putting things in writing is going to help your client become more flexible. It is a sign of brain disease and diminished capacity.

## SUCCEED WITH SENIOR CLIENTS

**5. Calculation Problems**

You may not catch this problem unless you set it up with a client to check out your suspicions of her difficulty in this area. For example, you take a college-educated client to lunch, and when the check comes you ask her to calculate the tip. If she can't do it, or defers to you or avoids the subject, that is a clue for you. Most educated people know how to calculate a tip.

Or if you ask a client to give you some direct feedback on a statement you show her as to whether her investments have gained or lost value, and she seems clueless as to your question, that may be another indication of calculation problems. She can't compare a starting number to a current one. You would say, now that you see this statement, can you tell whether you gained or lost anything? If you show her the starting number, the value at the beginning and the value at the end of the statement period, and she can't tell you if there is a difference between the two (assuming there is a difference!), she may be demonstrating a calculation problem. She can't add or subtract the two numbers.

**6. Disorientation**

Medical personnel check a patient's orientation in what we call three spheres: time, place and person. Your client probably knows who he is. When that orientation is gone, your client is in serious trouble!

Does she know today's date or the day of the week? Those are simple questions you can ask. Does she know the time of day? If she looks at a watch, does she understand how to tell time?

An important indication of orientation problems is getting lost going to a familiar place. If your client who has been to see you numerous times in the past can't find her way to your office or meeting place, that is also an important clue. Getting lost going on a familiar route, like the way home, is also a clue.

## SUCCEED WITH SENIOR CLIENTS

### EMOTIONAL SIGNS
**1. Unusual emotional distress**
These may be some of the more obvious signs of trouble for you to spot in your interactions with your aging client. If your client is very upset ("freaking out," to put it in slang terms), persistently distressed, anxious or does not respond to questions you are asking, this can be an indicator of diminished ability to stay focused. Going through a wide range of emotions in a brief conversation may also be a sign of trouble, such as quickly moving from laughing to crying and back again.

**2. Being inappropriate emotionally for the circumstances**
A client may express emotions that are out of whack with what is being talked about. For example, if a client has been forced to give up living independently and is sad about it but is laughing and smiling while saying it is sad, that is inappropriate for the subject. Some people with cognitive impairment are unable to modulate their emotions or realize that they are inappropriate. If it doesn't seem right to you in just talking over finances with your client, pay attention. Something may indeed not be right.

### BEHAVIORAL SIGNS
**1. Mental health red flags**
Changes in the brain that can indicate brain disease or mental health problems can show up in your interactions with a client. You may see the following.

### Delusions
A client who is fixated on things that are not true may be having what we call delusions. These are persistent false beliefs that sometimes emerge as fear that the person is being followed, spied on or tracked.

## Hallucinations

A person may also see, hear or smell things others around them do not. If you see your client talking to a person who is not there, that could be a sign of a hallucination or sensory experience that is not shared by others at that time. The experience is quite real to your client when this takes place, and you cannot talk him out of it with logic. Just note to yourself that he seems to be hearing or seeing things and record the date.

## 2. Unkempt appearance

A normally well-groomed client you are used to seeing well dressed comes to you with dirty clothing or seems to be unbathed. Her hair may not be combed or her attire is odd, such as two pairs of pants, or several layers of shirts or tops. If she smells as if she needs a bath, that is a clue something is wrong. This is another red flag to note and record.

These clues you find in your normal observation of your client are important over time. Dementia is always progressive. The capacity that is diminishing now will be worse the next time you see or speak with your client if the issue is dementia.

## Signs of Elder Abuse

In the above discussion, with highlights taken from the publication *Assessment of Older Adults With Diminished Capacity*, the handbook does not connect elder financial abuse with the other signs or red flags. However, we want you, as an advisor, to include financial elder abuse in your observations. It is something every advisor needs to look for. We devote Chapter 3 in this book to that subject, and we also believe that it, of itself, may also be a sign of diminished capacity. This is not always so, as perfectly competent people also fall victim to elder abuse. However, if a client reports being taken advantage of financially, or that a family member or other is manipulating the older person, be on the alert. This is another possible sign that your client has diminished capacity.

There are two main ways that financial elder abuse could come to your attention. The first is a direct report by your aging client or by a family member who reports a problem to you. For example, your client's son calls you to report that Dad has been giving money to Internet scammers. This is definitely an alarming sign of possible diminished capacity. You must not ignore it or dismiss it as "the family's problem." It is everyone's problem. There are things you can do, discussed in detail in Chapters 3 and 6. The second way financial elder abuse could come to your attention is when you note sudden and unusual changes in your client's account. This could include large and unexplained withdrawals. Your client had been stable in his spending and his need to withdraw funds prior to that.

It could include odd requests by your client to wire funds to unknown and suspicious addresses. Or it could include an unexplained change in the persons authorized to access the account.

Older people, particularly those who have diminished capacity, are easy prey for thieves, scammers and manipulators, both within their own families and from outsiders. Signs of elder abuse, presented directly by your client, who tells you about it, or indirectly, by what you see going on in the client's account, should be acted on promptly and through a planned process. If you do not yet have a clear protective policy for aging clients to keep them from being abused, that is a step you must take. You need to have a plan detailing how to stop abuse that may be under way. We provide a sample plan for you in this book.

## When a Supposed Red Flag Means Something Other Than Diminished Capacity

Other factors may be at work that could explain your client's behavior when you first see anything that you suspect may be a red flag. There are factors besides dementia that can cause behavior changes in your client. The difference between a red flag and another outside factor is that the red flags can lead to permanent change, while the outside things, such as stresses, may go away with time. Stresses can arise from changes in a person's life that are both expected and unexpected.

**Major life events,** such as death of a spouse, are devastating to just about everyone. These events cause extreme stress and will at least temporarily throw a client off balance. Of course you want to ask your client what is going on in her life when you converse and you want to find out about recent major stressful events. Grief, and an extended grieving process after losing a loved one, is an important consideration. As people age, they experience these losses more and more often. Consider how that will affect your dealings with them. It may not be the right time to make decisions if a person is distraught over a major life event.

A client going through such a process as grieving is what can be called a "mitigating factor," which would explain behavior that otherwise doesn't seem normal for the individual you know. Other mitigating factors may be at work as well. We do not want to jump to conclusions too quickly that a person has cognitive impairment, and resulting diminished capacity, without some inquiry into whether anything else can be affecting the client's mental status. Consider these other possibilities.

## Medication and Medical Treatment

If you have ever, yourself, taken a medication of any kind and had an unexpected effect from it, you know that medications can wreak havoc on a person's mental and physical status. People react differently to medications, and results of anything given to an older person can vary. Medication and medical conditions can also temporarily alter a person's mental status to the point that they seem more confused than usual, less able to make decisions, or otherwise "out of it. "If you encounter this problem, the best way to handle it is to ask your client, gently and respectfully, about what you see.

For example, if a client seems unable to track the conversation you are having with him, you can say, "Jack, you seem a little under the weather today. Is there anything unusual going on?" You might say, "How's your health right now?" You can ask about family or what he's been doing with his time lately.

If you are concerned that these questions are none of your business, or that it's your job to just manage money and you don't need to dig into personal affairs, we can only urge you to change your thinking. Money is as personal as it gets. How the person's life is going along is your business if you want to keep your client financially safe. Sizing up factors that could account for a client's red flags is part of your job. If someone just had major surgery a week ago and is taking pain medication every few hours, it's not the time to ask her to make a major decision. She may be temporarily under too much stress, or too fuzzy in her thinking, to do that. And what looks at first like a red flag may just be a temporary condition explained by her recent surgery, medication change or loss of a loved one.

## Physical Impairments as Factors That Affect What You Observe in Your Client

Other mitigating factors besides life events and medication changes that look like red flags but are not can include physical changes your client goes through with aging. Loss of physical ability is normal as we age. Wear and tear on the body over time usually result in loss of strength and function. Likewise, common physical health problems, such as arthritis, cause pain. Chronic pain is very distracting. A person experiencing it may have trouble concentrating that is unrelated to any brain changes brought on by dementia. She may appear to you to be unable to concentrate, and you may think this is a red flag. But when you speak with your client and learn more about her physical status, you may learn that she has a health issue that causes pain, and that until her medication relieves it, it is not a good time for you to have a conversation with her.

If this list of possible other causes for what appear to be red flags sounds confusing, it is. With aging, there may be multiple factors at work creating the picture you have of your client at any given moment. The point is to simply consider them. Ask yourself if anything else might be an explanation for why your client can't seem to follow the conversation. Consider what can happen if your client is misjudged to be less than competent when the truth might be that she really is just having a bad day.

Physical factors play a part in how you see your client and how your client responds to your efforts to transact business with her. Common issues you will likely experience in observing your client's responses to you may be these.

**Hearing loss**

Thirty percent of adults 65-74 years old, and 47% of adults 75 years old or older, have a hearing impairment.[10] It is likely that some of your older clients will not be able to hear as well as you'd like them to. Sometimes blank stares or inappropriate responses from older clients to the things you are asking about do

---

[10] National Institutes of Health, Hearing Loss, http://nihseniorhealth.gov/hearingloss/hearinglossdefined/01.html. (last accessed 8.3.15)

not indicate cognitive problems like dementia. Rather, it could mean that the older person can't hear clearly and either does not wear a hearing aid or the hearing aid is not helpful. It is a common problem that elders who need them do not necessarily embrace the idea of wearing a hearing aid.

Medicare does not cover the cost of hearing aids, and, for some people, that is a barrier to getting one. The cost is normally thousands of dollars out of pocket. In addition, the hearing aid may symbolize something the elder fears: getting old and losing control of his life. Or he may find it embarrassing to wear a device. In any case, if your client is not catching on to what you are saying or asking, it is good to simply ask if she can hear you well. As the problem of diminished hearing is so common, and the risk rises with age, be careful about assuming that a client has diminished capacity until you have at least asked the question about hearing loss as a factor in what you see.

**Fatigue/limited stamina**
Your authors have worked with aging adults over a period of years, and we have both observed that it is common for many older people to have more energy and to be more alert at certain times of the day compared with other times. Some are most alert in the morning, so it is best to have a conversation with them then. Others don't feel really awake until afternoon. For them it's more beneficial to have serious conversations at their best time of day. The only way to learn what works for your aging client is to ask. You might say, "What time of day is best for me to call you?" or something to that effect. They'll probably be able to tell you, and you can then eliminate fatigue, grogginess or lack of alertness as factors as to why your conversation with the individual may not be going well. Memory loss, or the ability to process information, will likely seem much more of an issue

when a person is fatigued. Again, be cautious about jumping to conclusions that a person has diminished capacity when you are having difficulty communicating with her. Be sure there aren't other factors complicating your observation of the client's cognitive ability.

Additional mitigating factors can explain a client's behavior that may suggest cognitive impairment, but it may be something else.

## Slow processing of your words

A younger person may be able to catch on more quickly to new information than an older person, as we typically are slower to think through information as we age. Of course everyone ages differently, and there are plenty of exceptions. However, as we age, our brains don't usually work as fast as they once did. This has nothing to do with intelligence or with how clearly a person can think. It may be explained by the fact that with many years of life experience, we have a lot of memories to sort through, and a lot of things are stored there in our brains. Older people have to sort them, and this can take longer than it might for another, younger person.

Although slow processing of information may also be part of the picture of dementia, it is important to be as patient as possible with your aging clients and to give them time to think through and respond to what you are saying. You will need to keep in mind that on the one hand, slow response from a client could possibly signal an inability to process new information, one hallmark of dementia. On the other hand, it might just be that a person is taking longer than you think it should take to get to an answer, and it's only because of an aging brain that may still be thinking clearly and fine. How can you tell which it is, a sign of dementia or just taking longer because of age? A single conversation or encounter will not provide the answer. You need repeated contact with the client to see how one day compares with another.

Slow processing may be connected to memory loss, and that is a clue dementia is playing a role. When you see evidence that your client can't recall a recent interaction, coupled with slow response to any direct question you ask, this leans more in favor of thinking the client may be impaired.

A cognitively intact older adult may forget your recent interaction but will remember later, especially if reminded. An impaired adult may have no recall at all of a conversation that took place yesterday or last week. A reminder won't help them recall it, and if they seem slow to catch on to what you are saying on top of that, you may reasonably conclude you are seeing a developing capacity issue. That observation needs to be compared with any other signs that suggest the client would not be able to understand her finances enough to make a decision.

## SUMMARY

In this chapter you have learned about the extent of our aging population and how aging affects risk to clients who are making financial decisions. You now know how to describe dementia and Alzheimer's disease in general terms.

Every advisor needs to recognize the red flags that can signal diminished capacity, and we walked you through cognitive signs, emotional signs, behavioral signs and signs of elder abuse. You also learned that some mitigating factors can explain behaviors clients demonstrate and that these may suggest a client does not, in fact, have diminished capacity. We encourage adopting a **best practice** of using a balanced approach to looking for the red flags we have enumerated above. First, recognize the red flags themselves. Next, ask yourself whether there may be any other reasonable explanation for what you see, other than a change in your client's brain, that is a sign of diminishing capacity for finances. Note these observations as you would document anything important with your clients. As we explain in the next chapters, your observations over time will give you a broader picture of what is going on with your client, and these observations become your guide as to what actions you should take to keep your client safe.

In Appendix 1, we offer you a checklist to help you remember the warning signs, or red flags, of diminished capacity.

# 2
# NUTS AND BOLTS: WHAT ARE THE COMPONENTS OF FINANCIAL CAPACITY?

**INTRODUCTION**
In this chapter we go into greater detail about how financial capacity is different from other kinds of capacity, and how hard it is to see diminished financial capacity in a client when first meeting her. It is a complex subject.

As a financial professional, you deal with complex subjects regularly. We do not want you to be intimidated by this one. We want you to finish this chapter with a better understanding of the depth of financial capacity and a respect for how baffling it can be for anyone to figure out if a person still has it, or has really lost, that capacity. This issue is a tough one for everyone, including lawyers, judges, doctors and family members. It is our belief that the more we understand financial decision-making capacity, the better we are at being able to figure out if it's time to stop a client from making decisions.

**The Common Yet Dangerous Assumptions We Make**
For any financial professional the difficulty of deciding whether a person can make financial decisions often leads to a dangerous assumption. The assumption is that, if the client doesn't

seem "out of it," he has financial capacity and you can proceed with this aging person just as you would with any other client.

This is dangerous not only because the client may lack sufficient judgment about risks to make the decisions you need him to make but also because mistakes on your part in assuming that an aging person is fine can come back to haunt you after your client passes. If he does obviously irrational things with his money to the point that he destroys a significant part of his wealth, his family may look to you for retribution. If their inheritance is affected, they may come after those who allowed blatantly dangerous things to go on without any effort to protect the client. ("How could you have let him *do* that???")

As regulators make it clear that you need senior-specific policies and that you should protect clients who are vulnerable, it may be hard to find an excuse when you have done nothing to protect a client who is clearly irresponsible regarding making financial decisions.

**Illustration: Sudden Change in Spending for a Frail, Elderly Client**
For example, imagine that a 95-year-old man, now frail, accustomed to being a conservative spender his entire adult life, is your client. He tells you he needs more cash right now because he wants to buy a house for his girlfriend. You can immediately comply, liquidate some of his assets to produce the cash he wants, or you can spend some time evaluating him and questioning his decision.

**What You Should Consider**
The 95-year-old client is at risk for dementia because of advanced age. He is asking you to depart from his long-established spending pattern of taking out a reasonable monthly draw for a comfortable life and now he suddenly wants to do something out

of character. In addition, you suspect that his girlfriend, much younger and without means of her own, is trying to manipulate your client. All of these factors should influence your decision about what to do in response to your client's request.

What you also should think about is the effect of the lavish gift on a younger woman by a 95-year-old in terms of what his family (heirs) might do when they find out about this. Is his desire to buy a house with cash for a girlfriend a warning sign of elder abuse? It could be. On the one hand, perhaps he is totally sharp and thinks he is in love with the younger woman. He wants to give her this wonderful gift while he can. But conversely, his adult children could see this as your aiding and abetting a financial abuser and expect you to be aware of his general condition.

Every person who develops any kind of dementia is vulnerable to financial manipulation and abuse. Every person developing dementia, even at the earliest stage, when you can just see an emerging problem with short-term memory, has brain cells that are being destroyed. This makes the person a sitting duck for any predator who wants to take advantage of him.

This is exactly where a protective, office-wide senior-specific policy comes in. If you had been regularly doing a review of your client's portfolio annually or every six months, along with your review of his cognitive status, you would be able to see changes that occur over time. (We explain how to put all these things to work in Chapter 6.)

## Tracking the Red Flags

A 95-year-old might be showing subtle red flags when you talk to him at these regular intervals. If you used a checklist derived from the descriptions above (or in Appendix 1) and reviewed it over the last two years, you might see that he had a couple of cognitive signs of diminished capacity both times you did your reviews. You might find that he was not able to follow the conversation once or twice. You might find that he was forgetful and didn't remember that he had already called you earlier, then called you a second time asking the same questions later the same day. With use of your standardized checklist, you have data to track. You note that the instances of red flags had gone up over those two years.

If these subtle signs of erosion of his memory or thought are on your radar, it is time to check in with the person to whom you escalate problematic matters. This needs another set of eyes.

Perhaps the other reviewer of the issue will not think it is anything to worry about. On the other hand, the other reviewer could see this as a dangerous situation, which looks like financial abuse, and the next step in your escalation policy should then take place.

As you can imagine, without a way to track problematic behavior or signs with your aging clients, you are stuck with having to suddenly make important decisions without a plan. Many advisors would simply give the client hundreds of thousands of dollars, as requested, and use the worn-out excuse: "I was just doing what my client asked, and that's what I have to do." We disagree.

The regulators want you to do better than blindly following client requests when red flags may be pointing to potential abuse. And the 95-year-old's heirs may want to hold you accountable for not taking protective action when FINRA and the SEC have put it in writing that the industry needs to create protective senior-specific policies. If you had such a policy, you would have the authority to contact a third party, perhaps one of your client's heirs who was appointed to this role, and talk it over. Chances are the heirs don't want their frail and vulnerable father giving away hundreds of thousands of dollars to a questionable girlfriend. They may be in a position to stop the gift, intervene through discussion, seek a psychological evaluation or take other protective action.

For clients who have no adult children, or no one paying attention to monitor their behavior, the risk of abuse is exceptionally high. This sort of single elderly person is a prime target for predators, as they believe they will get away with their manipulation and crimes, and, sadly, they often do. But when there is family, there is at least a chance that one of them will be authorized to take control of the account and protect the aging parent from being victimized.

## Creating Your Own Checklist

In our ongoing research on firms' practices, we have not seen a specific checklist for tracking diminished capacity. Therefore, we have created a quick-version checklist to help you get started in developing a comprehensive senior program for firms or offices. There is no rule provided by regulators that tells you what you must document regarding your own clients. You could put something together from the descriptions in this book, or you could create one from other sources that explain diminished capacity. As we have focused here on the essential elements you should be familiar with, you at least have a place to start. A "done for you" version of a more standardized and comprehensive checklist, together with a path for escalation and document to address the privacy issue, is available in the AgingInvestor.com program initiator template.[11]

Whichever form you use, be sure that everyone in the office labels and documents problematic behavior the same way and defines it the same way, so as to be uniform in your approach.

---

[11] Ten Step Program Initiator for protecting aging investors, http://www.aginginvestor.com/ten-step-policy-development-template-for-protecting-aging-investors/.

That allows you to collaborate with colleagues on deciding what to do and when to escalate a matter of diminished capacity. It also allows compliance personnel, or an internal senior-knowledgeable committee to whom a matter is escalated, the opportunity to make a reasoned decision based on use of common language descriptors. Following a reasoned and protective process is exactly what the regulators expect of you.

## Don't Clients Have a Right to Do What They Want With Their Own Money?

Of course everyone has the right to make his or her own financial decisions, but that assumes the person is competent to understand those decisions. The decisions a person has a right to make do not have to be logical or make sense to others. They *do* have to be understood by the person making those decisions, and that is where the difficult question of financial capacity comes into play. Is the older person who might possibly be impaired acting **in his own best interests**? Are the decisions consistent with his long-established values and beliefs?

There is an old saying, "There's no law against stupid decisions." It is true, as people make bad decisions every day. You probably have some clients who have this going on, and you struggle to help them be smarter about their finances. Or you at least try to keep them from losing too much with decisions you recommend against.

How can you tell if your client is just making dumb choices or if she is impaired with some physical problem that affects her judgment? It is not an easy call. But it is also possible to get data to help you make the call.

There are several ways, with psychological instruments, to measure financial capacity. Let us look at what researchers call financial capacity.

## Definition of Financial Capacity

Financial capacity is defined as **"the capacity to manage money and financial assets in ways that meet a person's needs and which are consistent with his/her values and self-interest."**[12] This seems straightforward, but it is not. Some people develop brain disease as they age, and with dementia, the erosion of mental capacity can take place over years. During the earliest stages of dementia, the brain cells are being damaged by the disease process, but the person has other brain cells "in reserve" and can still function in many areas without impairment. However, we have a body of scientific research now that has found that for people who are developing Alzheimer's disease, financial capacity is already impaired even at the beginning stage. By the time someone has "moderate" or middle-stage Alzheimer's disease, his financial capacity is already *significantly* impaired.[13]

At the earliest stages of Alzheimer's or other forms of dementia, the person may seem quite normal. She can still cook, drive, manage a home and pay her bills. But the first signs of memory loss emerge when she forgets that she has paid a bill and pays it twice. She starts to have trouble keeping her train of thought. She may not be able to calculate the price of an item when it is 20% off. These smaller signs are often dismissed by family as "just getting old." But dementia is *not* a normal part of aging. Rather, it is a progressive problem that gradually robs the person of the ability to keep track of money altogether. Normal aging does not cause a decline in basic intelligence. Brain disease, on the other hand, changes how a person is able to think and keep track of things, including money.

---

[12] http://www.asaging.org/blog/financial-capacity-aging-society. (last accessed 5.12.16)

[13] http://archneur.jamanetwork.com/article.aspx?articleid=776646.

Memory loss is often the first warning sign of dementia. Short-term memory is affected even when long-term memory may be entirely intact for some time. Forgetting things, appointments, directions and objects are often what families may notice first. Forgetting bills is a red flag that you, as an advisor, may not see personally, but it is something to ask your client about. Acting in one's own best interests is not consistent with failing to pay one's bills. A person who cannot keep track of or pay bills for herself is a person with a significant limitation in her financial capacity.

One reason you, a financial professional, must be acutely aware of signs of diminished capacity is that your client can get into financial trouble very easily when his capacity for decisions is diminishing. As it is a process rather than a single event, no alarm bells sound loudly at any one point in typical development of dementia. You may not get anything other than subtle warning signs or puzzling changes in the way your client interacts with you.

In view of those subtle warning signs, if you treat the person as if he is perfectly fine, you make no adjustments in how often you review his portfolio and you have no plan for what happens next in his possible development of brain disease, trouble lurks for you and your client. A sudden request or change can occur, leaving you in a stressful and dangerous situation with your client. Your client may be unable to understand the need for any change in his portfolio and you need permission you are unable to get. This can lead to unnecessary losses. Losses can then multiply when your client can no longer appreciate the need for decisions you want him to make. If you choose to escalate the matter after your client can no longer give you permission to take necessary steps to manage the portfolio, it may be too late.

## How Can an Advisor Ever Figure Out if a Client Has Diminished Financial Capacity?

As defined above, we know that a person with capacity will act in her own best interests. The ability to do this represents a broad continuum of activities and skills, which neuropsychologist and lawyer Dr. Daniel Marson, a leading researcher, has defined as being divided into nine areas, or domains. If you consider all of these when you communicate with your client, you have the best chance of determining if your client is impaired. When there is doubt, evaluation by a doctor can be very helpful in giving you additional data.

## The Nine Distinct Areas of Financial Capacity

Dr. Marson and his team of researchers have developed descriptions for the broad continuum of activities and skills that make up this kind of capacity.[14] They describe the areas in the following ways.

### 1. Basic money skills
This includes the ability to identify coins and currency as well as to identify the relative worth of currency. It also includes the ability to accurately count and sort currency.

### 2. Financial conceptual knowledge
This involves broader concepts of finances, such as what a money market is and how a home equity loan works. Does the client understand the basic concept of any kind of loan?

### 3. Cash transactions
This involves understanding the cost of an item, how much to pay and a price increase or reduction. A person with this area intact would be able to accurately pay the charge for a purchase.

### 4. Checkbook management
A person who has this area intact can use a checkbook and register, as well as understand online banking, if that is used in

---

[14] http://www.ncbi.nlm.nih.gov/pmc/articles/PMC2714907/. (last acccessed 5.12.16)

lieu of paper checks. This area involves understanding charges against an account.

**5. Bank statement management**

This skill involves identifying a bank or financial institution statement. It includes being able to find the balance, reconcile a statement, and determine where to find the recorded deposits and withdrawals.

**6. Financial judgment**

This involves understanding value of any financial transaction or proposal. A person with intact financial judgment would know how to get paid and how to correct an error in payment. He would be able to spot an obvious scam and perceive an offer that was too good to be true as phony.

**7. Bill payment**

A person who is intact in this area understands her bills, current budget and money she may owe. She is able to question errors and knows the consequences of an unpaid bill.

**8. Knowledge of personal assets and estate**

This means that the person understands his annual income, where it comes from and how much he generally has in overall assets. This knowledge need not be precise but should be basically accurate.

**9. Investment decision-making**

The person who has this area intact is able to engage in and actively participate in developing an understanding of any financial investment decision. Knowing the value of a proposed transaction and the attendant risks are part of this area of competency.

If this sounds complicated, it is. You may be wondering if *any* of your clients are essentially competent in all nine areas. Some are not. Most people, if you wanted to take the time involved to patiently explain things like risk of an investment in simple terms, would get it. But when a client can't tell the difference between a twenty-dollar bill and a five-dollar bill, that client is not competent financially, even if he can carry on a perfectly normal conversation about his favorite sports team or politics.

Here are two ways to see if your client has any losses in an area of financial capacity listed above: cash transactions.

If you have the opportunity to take your client to lunch, do so and ask him to calculate the tip on the bill. If he can't do it, he has a problem and may not be intact in all nine areas.

Next, ask your client about her personal bill-paying at home. Does she use online banking? You might ask her to show you how she accesses her account and pays bills. Many seniors do not use the Internet or online banking. For those clients, you might start a conversation about how they keep track of bills that are due and find out whether he has ever paid a bill twice or is forgetting any of the bills lately. If a client tells you that a son or daughter is doing this chore for them, there is usually a reason for it. That gives you another piece of information to consider in figuring out if your client still has financial capacity.

**Illustration**

Rhonda called asking for an appointment, worried that her mother was being taken advantage of by an organization that kept asking her for money. She had gotten lost going home from a meeting, and the police had to find her and take her home just last week. She had left the stove on at home, and Rhonda found out about it. Fortunately a neighbor stopped by and turned off the stove. Rhonda thought her mother might have dementia.

Co-author Dr. Davis does testing for diminished capacity for clients, and Rhonda wanted her mother tested. Likewise, she wanted to know if her mother really knew what she was doing, giving money to the organization every time they asked, in ever-larger sums. The determination as to whether a person has capacity for certain decisions is a legal one, often made by lawyers and, sometimes, by judges. The lawyers and judges do rely on medical information and psychological reports to help them decide if a person has capacity for financial decision-making.

As a part of the analysis, and to help Rhonda figure out what to do about her mother, I interviewed Rhonda's mother in my office. I asked her about the organization that was regularly pursuing her for large donations. She said she had been writing checks for them over most of her life. Wondering if she did have knowledge of her assets and her estate (Area 8, above), I asked her if she knew how much it cost her to live each month. She answered accurately, which I knew because Rhonda had told me about her expenses. She had savings, but she was not what one would call wealthy.

I then asked her if she knew how much she had in savings. She was not able to provide an answer. Instead, she said, *"There is no possibility I could ever run out of money. None whatsoever."*

Privately, Rhonda told me that this was certainly not true, that her mother was probably going to need to move out of her apartment, as she was not safe to be there alone any longer. Rhonda said that her mother had less than a million dollars, and that the cost of long-term care for her was going to rise sharply. She had income, but as the expense of caregiving was added, she would have to use her assets to pay for it.

She was tested by Dr. Davis and found to have very significant memory loss issues. He recommended that she not be allowed to make any more financial decisions, especially about donations to the organization she had been connected to over many years.

Here is a summary of the signs of diminished financial capacity and general capacity that Rhonda and her mom's financial advisor should have noted and acted upon.

## SUCCEED WITH SENIOR CLIENTS

**1. Getting lost going home.** A person who becomes disoriented en route to a familiar place is a person with at least one sign of diminished capacity—**confusion.**
**2. Leaving the stove on at home.** This is not only a danger sign, it is also generally another sign of diminished capacity—**memory loss.**
**3. Inability to recognize the size of her estate.** She thought she could never run out of money, yet she was not so wealthy that this was actually the case. This is another sign of diminished financial capacity.
**4. Unusually large withdrawals from her savings.** She was making larger and larger donations to the organization. This could be a sign of **possible financial abuse.**

### Red Flags for the Advisor to Note

The progressively larger checks to an organization the client had contributed to for years were a sign of change, because the amounts had gone from a few thousand dollars a year to $100,000. **The large withdrawals were a departure from an established pattern and should have alerted the advisor to an issue.** It was indeed abuse, as the organization was taking advantage of her memory loss and her confusion. Likewise, they probably knew from talking to her by phone, which was how they asked for donations, that she was not "all there."

Yes, individuals do have the right to do what they want with their money, but there is a line to be drawn when the giving reaches the point of creating financial danger for that person. Taken in the context of her memory loss and confusion, this elder was not acting in her own best interests. That is, the distinction between charitable giving based on sound decisions and decision-making that is impaired.

## Measuring Financial Capacity With Testing

In the case of Rhonda's mother, age 84, there was no question in Rhonda's mind that her mother was impaired. But people vary in their ability to express competency from day to day and, sometimes, at different points within a day. Some people probably thought the elder was fine. It is easy to be fooled, by an older person's congenial and socially appropriate conversation, into thinking this means the person is cognitively intact. "Normal" conversation does not tell us much about a person's financial capacity.

We get clues over time from our own observations about clients, but it can be very helpful if there is also objective data to help answer the question as to whether a person is competent to make financial decisions.

In the case of Rhonda's mother, she was still going to meetings and lived independently at the time the question of possible financial abuse came up. We recommended testing, to provide her with something objective to use with the organization, which was going to object to being cut off from a steady source of financial donations.

## What Is Neuropsychological Testing?

Neuropsychological testing (using groups of related paper and pencil and verbal question-and-answer tests) can provide useful information to take the question of capacity outside the realm of speculation. Compare that with the personal opinions of family, other professionals, acquaintances and social contacts of an elder, who may all have differing opinions as to whether or not a person has capacity for financial decisions. Test data provides numbers, scores, something specific.

This kind of testing can give useful data about which tested parts of a person's cognitive function do or do not compare normally with the tested function of people of similar age and education. While some slowing of mental processing is expected with age, many brain functions remain normal in normal aging. When a person falls below a measure of what is normal, and we have testing scores to tell us where and how, it can give us guidance about whether to allow a person to keep making financial decisions.

In Rhonda's case she had a durable power of attorney document for her mother, which she had the right to use to stop her mother from draining away her savings by giving it to the organization. Her mother loved to give money away, as it made her feel good. Testing showed how impaired her mother was, and it made Rhonda's decision much easier.

We contacted the organization and asked them to address the issue of the increasing donations. They immediately stopped asking the elder for money, perhaps fearing legal action.

In this case testing was a crucial part of the picture, which gave everyone involved a definitive direction.

### How Does This Affect You?

We recommend you suggest neuropsychological testing when you have a client who is in a sort of "grey zone" between competence and incompetence. If you are concerned, and you have seen some red flags suggesting impairment, this is an action you can take. Making the suggestion is one way to determine your client's willingness to let a professional address the apparent memory problem. This is a sensitive subject to bring up with any client.

Some language you might consider, depending on the client, would go like this.

**You:** "Bill, I've noticed over the past several months that you've had some trouble remembering our conversations. I've been keeping notes of what we talk about, as I always do, and I've seen a change. Are you noticing more problems with your memory lately?"

**Client:** "Well, yes, I'm getting older, and I forget things. That's true. It's normal for a person my age, isn't it?"

**You:** "Bill, it could be, but I have a concern here, because a lot of important decisions that I ask you to make depend on your remembering information. And I definitely don't want you to make any mistakes because of being forgetful. My job is to protect your money. I'm wondering if you'd be willing to get some basic memory testing so we can get a better handle on this memory question. What do you think about that?"

**Client:** (Ideal response!) Okay, I guess that would be all right. Where do I go to get that?

At this point you can suggest that the client either go to his own physician and ask for a referral to a psychologist who can do the kind of testing needed, or you can suggest some vetted professionals in the client's area, if you know of reputable ones who can do the work needed.

## Resistance

Not every client will embrace the idea of having his memory tested. Some elders who are suffering from memory loss are aware that they are losing their memories and do everything they can to hide it. Or a spouse hides it and covers for them. They fear losing control over their lives, and their fear is well-founded. By cleverly changing the subject, avoiding the things they can't remember and the questions they can't answer, they manage for some time to continue giving the appearance of normal function. However, their cognitive ability and capacity for financial judgment is impaired.

The client could get angry, insulted or otherwise reject your suggestion. If that happens, it's time to involve the family member closest to the elder. One hopes that you have a relationship with a family member or trusted other close to the client. If you have your client's permission, you can bring this up with the family member and work on getting an evaluation done on your client. Leaving the client to his or her own devices, or waiting "until something happens," is unwise. It sets up the client for poor decisions, or even for financial disaster.

The client may be partially competent for some things but incompetent for financial decisions, particularly those that involve evaluating risk or assessing an overall strategy. This is the nature of loss of capacity. Its onset is insidious. It creeps up slowly and is not obvious at first. A smooth and socially appropriate exterior may mask the true nature of cognitive impairment developing beneath the surface. The loss of capacity is neither black nor white. It may be changeable and inconsistent for some time. There may be no clear answer to the question at any given point as to whether a person is competent.

This "grey zone" is a very dangerous time for a person who is developing dementia. Predators love people in this condition. They sound all right, and therefore everyone around them allows them to continue as if they could think through financial decisions with all their areas of capacity intact. However, they cannot appreciate risk. They are subject to things like "front door fraud," when a scammer knocks on the door and offers to do work. The elder is persuaded to do it. The scammer either takes a very inflated sum in advance, or gets paid in advance and does not do the work, then disappears.

Likewise, financial scams abound with people in this "grey zone" before it becomes apparent to all—advisors, family, doctors and friends—that the elder should not be making financial decisions. The TV, the newspaper and the Internet are all sources the elder may see, and "great deals" beckon, because the older person can't discern a scam. The truth is that scammers know elders generally tend to be more gullible than younger people, and they exploit this ruthlessly. Even completely competent seniors are more likely than younger people to be taken advantage of because there is a tendency of the older generation, sometimes called "the handshake generation," to trust someone who seems nice and speaks politely.

**Action Steps**

Advisors serve their aging clients best if they are conscious of the need to watch for the signs of diminished capacity. If you are concerned, suggest testing. Seek out and get to know some competent psychologists and neuropsychologists in your client's area, or learn how to get a reliable referral to someone. If your client's doctor is not helpful, seek other resources. Many counties, particularly in larger urban and surrounding suburban areas, have professional organizations with lists of psychologists and neuropsychologists posted on their websites. If you do not know your local resources, the American Psychological Association is a place to start http://www.apa.org/.

On the organization's website there is a "find a psychologist" menu. There, you can find someone in your client's area, under the specialty "neuropsychology." Though this feature is designed for a consumer seeking a therapist, it can lead you to those who practice in the area and who do testing. Most psychologists will call you back if you leave a message with a clear description of what you want. If you go this route, ask for **someone who can test an aging person for memory loss and signs of dementia.** That is a start, at least if you do not have a way to obtain a recommendation from someone you know.

Many counties have their own psychological professional associations. Do a search in your own area or your client's area for listings. You can direct concerned family members to local resources and encourage them to check out listings and reputations of those who hold themselves out as trained in doing the necessary testing for capacity. If you do not know a qualified psychologist or neuropsychologist, be straightforward with your client but help them learn how to find the information they need. Many people are simply unaware that psychological testing can tell us a great deal about a person's ability to make financial decisions.

You will, of course, need your client's permission to learn the test results. It can be very helpful to work with your client's family members on such an effort. They may assist you in persuading the client to get memory testing to help all of you.

## What Other Options Do You Have for Clients With Diminished Capacity?

Perhaps you have no one in your client's world to help you. Widowed persons with diminished capacity, with no children, are at particular risk, as you may not have identified any trusted third party to call when you are concerned. There is no family.

### Using Fiduciaries

An ideal way to address this, one we consider to be a **best practice**, is to require your aging client to identify a friend or trusted other or a professional fiduciary as that third party for you to call when necessary. If she does not know anyone trustworthy, aging organizations, nonprofits serving the elderly and legal organizations serving elders may either provide a professional fiduciary or refer you to one in the area. In our state, California, fiduciaries must pass a qualification test and be licensed. That provides at least some measure of security against fiduciary abuse. However, with any situation in which an unmonitored person handles large sums for an incompetent one, there is a risk of abuse even from those who are licensed. We advocate having another person, perhaps the financial professional, to oversee the actions of a fiduciary appointed to manage the daily finances of an impaired elder.

Fiduciaries also serve as conservators or guardians, appointed by the courts, to take over financial and personal responsibility for vulnerable and incompetent elders when a court finds them incompetent and there is no family to fill the conservator or guardian role. Sometimes the trust department of the client's bank is the most trusted resource for finding a fiduciary.

For most people it is safer, and better, to have someone they know and trust serve in that capacity rather than have a complete stranger do the job. Arranging for someone to take over for an individual should they become incapacitated is part of every good estate plan. The appointed person would be the successor trustee if there is a trust or the agent on the client's durable power of attorney document. Unfortunately, not everyone does estate planning, even if they have high net worth. Estate planning attorneys will tell you that fewer than half of all people in our country do, or complete, their estate planning.

A step you should be taking is to find out if your client has an appointed third party, particularly if he is widowed and has no children or family he can trust. If he does not have an appointed person, you can ask him to find one, urge him to take care of this and stay on that point until your client has complied. If you do not do so, you may lose that client to someone whom an appointed conservator, guardian or fiduciary likes to use as a financial advisor. They will have complete control should your client become incapacitated.

## Client Retention

If you insist that every client identify a trusted other, and you work with your client to find and identify that person, with a backup individual as well, you have a much better chance of maintaining control over the client's assets. You want to communicate with the appointed person while your client is still competent and able to discuss why he or she was chosen and introduce the person to you. The appointed person at least has a connection to you, and you have an opportunity to explain what your client wants and her investment philosophy, ideally with your client present for this conversation. If you ignore this need for the third party and wait until a court or someone else takes decision-making power away from your client, the appointed person, be it a conservator, guardian or just a family member with legal authority, you are much more likely to lose the client.

And before you reach out to the third party with your observations about possible diminished capacity, should you escalate the matter within your organization? Is the compliance department more likely to give you a good solution that you can figure out for yourself?

## Escalation

Let's imagine that your client has diminished capacity right now. You are more than a little concerned. You need to make some adjustments to her portfolio, and you know she is so impaired, she can't even understand your questions any longer, much less answer them. You don't have an appointed third party in your file, because you just never thought of it. You know your client now has significant memory loss, and you don't want to count on her to make any decisions. If you don't make that adjustment in the portfolio, your client will suffer serious financial consequences.

## SUCCEED WITH SENIOR CLIENTS

You have a dilemma. If you take your chances and pretend that your client is capable of making investment decisions and do what seems right, there is no assurance that you will guess correctly. Things can go south, even with your best intentions. But without your client's permission to conduct any transaction, you are taking a risk that your client's heirs, whether they be distant relatives you've never heard of or not, will question you. Anyone with a right to inherit from your client may seriously question your choice to conduct any financial transaction, while knowing that your client was "out of it," when you suggested any changes to the portfolio. This can happen as well if you do not take reasonable steps to protect assets that any other advisor would take.

If your client suffers large losses, **heirs can scrutinize your conduct.** "Why did you let that happen? Didn't you *know* my father had dementia? Everyone else knew!" Potentially, they can take legal action against you for not doing what was reasonable with a client whom you should have known was impaired. They can complain to regulators, find a lawyer to take whatever legal action may be feasible and otherwise put under the microscope your choice to proceed with a client you knew had diminished capacity. You don't want that. You are now held to a fiduciary standard to do what is best for the client. Consider what will look best for the *impaired client*.

Most firms and organizations we have reviewed on the question of what they do with a client who has diminished capacity will say that they escalate the problem. And what happens afterward is that privacy concerns may thwart the intention to contact a third party. No one we have found so far in our informal research has devised a senior-specific policy that addresses how to obtain a client's permission to contact a trusted third party when the first signs of cognitive impairment surface. Escalating the matter then leads to getting rid of the client. Potential liability will always drive organizational decisions like this.

We think the financial services industry can do better than that. Terminating your clients because of diminished capacity puts them in a more vulnerable place than ever. Either they are entirely subject to being ripped off by any predator who happens along in their lives, or they will be taken on by a different advisor who has a more creative way to solve the problem of diminished capacity than you do.

**The Alternative**
Even without a specific policy in place for aging clients in an office, or larger organization, some advisors have already established a relationship with the client's family. When Mom begins to show signs of trouble, the family is prepared, and the successor on the family trust takes over the decision-making for Mom. There has been communication over a period of years, the advisor and the client's family know and trust each other, legal documents are in place, and it can go smoothly. We have spoken with advisors who do this as a matter of course, and they tell us this intergenerational conversation with the involved advisor works very well. This is not, though, how things typically work out across the country.

More likely, firms get rid of cognitively impaired clients when impairment becomes obvious and no one has stepped up with legal authority over the client. Or the clients' adult children take over for the aging parent and immediately move assets away from the long-standing advisor that the parent had for many years. There was no relationship in place with the adult children. There was no agreement about what to do when Mom or Dad began showing the first signs of declining mental capacity. With longevity increasing and wealth being transferred by the trillions of dollars to aging Baby Boomers, the current model of how to address diminished capacity by terminating the client is going to result in devastating losses to financial firms. If you do not want this to be *you*, losing clients because of age-related problems, you will need a plan.

The plan is a new program in your office that anticipates that any client is at risk for diminished capacity. If you want to keep your clients for life, that life may include having a trusted third party in the overall strategy of how to manage assets as your clients age. Every new policy you adopt should consider the very real possibility of diminished capacity. Your plan should have a systematic way to address diminished capacity. It should also have built-in communication with adult children, or appointed fiduciaries, so that you can take appropriate protective action when you need to do so to keep your client as financially safe as you can.

**Policy-Driven Preparation and Actions**

We recommend development of senior-specific office policies for advisors and their firms, detailing the major components of such a policy in Chapter 6. If you have a clear policy for seniors in place, you will know what to do when your client begins to demonstrate diminished capacity. You will have an appointed person to contact when you are concerned about those red flags you see in your client. You will not only have the contact information in your file for the person to call "just in case" there is a capacity issue with your client but you will also have a document that gives you permission to make that call.

Having a plan in place to anticipate possible incapacity is not only sensible, it is protective of you, as well as your client. As no one can predict who will develop dementia, or other cognitive problems, and who will not, we have only the statistical likelihood to go on. Recall that the odds of developing Alzheimer's disease are at least one in three by the time your client reaches age 85. And remember, as well, that two-thirds of those diagnosed with Alzheimer's are women.

Every advisor needs to see every aging client as potentially in need of the protections that a senior-specific program can afford them. If a client begins to suffer memory problems in her 60s, and shows those red flags in her late 70s, it does not matter whether she has had a formal diagnosis of Alzheimer's or dementia, or not. Some people with dementia never do have an official diagnosis, but everyone around them realizes they are not okay.

The point here is not to wait for a diagnosis from any doctor to tell you what you must do. It is not at all proactive to wait until you have an impaired client to begin the process of developing a senior program in your office. You should have clear steps to follow, as a matter of course, when you see red flags and when financial decision-making is required from your client.

The usual helter-skelter approach to clients with diminished capacity that we see all around us in the industry is simply not working very well.

## SUMMARY

Financial capacity is a complex subject, with multiple dimensions, and is never easy to determine even for professionals who work with aging persons on a daily basis. Dr. Marson's decades of research tells us that there are nine distinct domains of financial capacity. A person must be functioning well in all nine areas to be considered fully financially competent. When your client seems to be declining in his capacity for financial decisions, you need to consider carefully whether he is truly capable of making the financial decisions you need him to make. You are exposed to potential legal challenges when you treat a client with diminished capacity for finances as if he were able to make serious money decisions. It may be unsafe to think that your client can appreciate the risks of any investment when he is impaired, even at the earliest stages of dementia. With all financial professionals handling retirement accounts now held to a fiduciary standard, you need to take into consideration that this standard puts an even heavier burden on you when you suspect your client no longer has financial capacity.

# 3

# FINANCIAL ELDER ABUSE: HOW YOU CAN FIGHT THE CRIME OF THE CENTURY

**INTRODUCTION**

Some have called financial abuse of seniors "the crime of the century." It is a pervasive problem, and it is growing steadily with our aging population. As you can discern from the prior chapter, people who do not have full financial capacity are at higher risk for abuse because they lack the judgment to see abuse as it is happening. They may fear retribution. They may be unwilling to report family members even if the senior knows that the family is abusing them. Most elder abuse is unreported, and most abusers get away with this crime.

This chapter is an effort to help you, the advisor, in your unique position of trust with your client to appreciate the extent of abuse in our country and to see how you can take a personal role in stopping abuse in its tracks. Can you solve this huge issue for every client? No. For some, you see it too late. For others, the client appears to be a willing victim and he allows the abuse. For certain clients, there is a stubborn unwillingness to give you permission to contact anyone who can stop the abuse. But for many clients, when you suspect abuse and see the warning signs we outline in this chapter, you will be able to be a kind of hero. You *can* stop financial abuse for them.

## How Big Is the Elder Abuse Problem?

According to a study by a private company, True Link Financial, the amount stolen from elders each year in our country is over $36 billion.[15] This includes not only outright theft by the unscrupulous people in their lives and the online predators who are after them but also other kinds of more subtle abuse.

Your older clients with dementia may lack the judgment to realize that someone offering to do a home repair worth $1,000, for example, is taking advantage of them by charging ten times the value of the job. The elder simply writes a check or gives a credit card, and the theft is hidden from view.

Your clients are not immune from financial abuse regardless of their education, sophistication or experience in financial matters. The True Link study had some surprising findings about the smart people who are financially abused. A significant number of victims are younger seniors, college-educated and not living in isolation.

They were the ones in the study who lost more money to abuse than those who were older, isolated and had less education.

Is financial abuse happening to YOUR clients right now? Of course it is. There is no escaping it. With a problem as big as this, no group of elders is immune. If you took a survey of your existing clients all age 65 or older, and asked them how many have ever been taken advantage of financially, you would be sure to get some clients who would admit to this. If you look at your own experience and count up any instance you know of,

---

[15] True Link Financial Report on Financial Elder Abuse. https://www.truelinkfinancial.com/news/latest-report-elder-financial-abuse-true-link-finds-36-48-billion-lost-annually-seniors/. (last accessed 5.12.16)

whether it is in your family, your neighborhood or your book of business, you will likely find some financial abuse as well.

## Why Is This Important for You?
The amounts stolen, fraudulently taken or just snatched from the unwary, are shocking. Remember that when your client loses assets, you lose fees. That is the most basic reason this should be important to you as a financial professional. Doing the right thing to keep your clients safe is certainly a motivator as well. It shows that you do care about them. And beyond that, the regulators are increasingly aware that financial professionals are in a position to take action and, sometimes, to stop and prevent financial abuse. They will soon get past merely urging you to take action and to report abuse. They will ultimately make it mandatory.

## Who Is Stealing From Your Aging Clients?
The most common rip-off artists are family. Sometimes they are the very trusted people your client appointed on a DPOA or to be the successor trustee of the family trust. Anyone who sees opportunity can commit financial abuse. It can come from some surprising sources, including charities, religious organizations and nonprofits.

Wealthy people we have personally met and worked with as clients have been abused by making "charitable" donations beyond their capacity to do so safely. Charities that have had longtime donors can turn into predators when a member of the organization or donor loses judgment about finances.

## Illustration
Marge is 86 and has dementia. She has been developing memory problems for five years, according to her family. She has been

wealthy all her life. She has always given large amounts to various charities, as well as spending freely on luxuries, travel and gifts for her relatives. She has a large trust, which pays for all of her expenses.

She was living in a community for seniors for three years, during which time her memory loss and financial judgment worsened. No one stepped in to put a stop to her lavish donations. A questionable charity hooked her on making monthly payments. Her financial advisor first suggested that she stop, then begged her to do so, as she gave away over $1 million in a short period of time. She either did not listen to him or she soon forgot what he said. He did not contact her daughter, who was a professional and her appointed person to serve as power of attorney.

By the time her donations exceeded a million dollars, and it became clear that she would need full-time caregiving, the advisor quit managing her account. He was frustrated, because his client would not listen to him.

Her daughter finally got involved and was able to control her mother's reckless spending, which Marge did not realize was reckless. She forgot what she had in the trust and how much was reasonable to donate, given her increasing care needs.

Marge will have enough to cover 24/7 care for her remaining years, but only because her daughter is now making decisions for her, in conjunction with the trustee.

Could this have been handled differently by the advisor who ultimately lost the client and quit in frustration?

Yes, it could have been done differently. Here are ways we think the advisor could have achieved a better outcome for himself.

**1.** He could have, and should have, had the daughter's contact information in his file from the beginning. He could have, and should have, obtained his client's permission to get in touch with the daughter and to share what was going on with her if he had concerns about his client's judgment.

**2.** He could have asked for the daughter's help to either take over control of the spending from the trust or to ask the daughter to have his client evaluated for dementia. The daughter, in fact, did so, realized how impaired her mother was and moved her mother in with her to provide the care the mother needed.

Taking those proactive steps might well have maintained the assets he managed under his watch. The daughter agreed with him that the donations to the charity were excessive in view of the total available to support her mother and her increasing long-term care needs. Legal authority existed in the form of the durable power of attorney to permit the daughter to stand in the shoes of her mother and make decisions for her. The mother, who trusted her daughter, was willing to take direction from her.

**The missing link to a better solution was the advisor.** He saw unusually large withdrawals, even for this wealthy client. He tried to reason with a person whose judgment was impaired about finances, and this, of course, is futile. He never contacted the daughter. He did nothing but plead with his cognitively impaired client to stop giving away so much money. That was his mistake. He no longer has the client or her assets to manage.

## What's the Takeaway From That Case?

People whose judgment is impaired by the brain changes of dementia are likely to do foolish or dangerous things with their money. An advisor can stand idly by, thinking, "It's her money, and she can do what she wants with it." Or the advisor can make a more prudent choice and ask oneself: "This doesn't look normal for this client. Is there a way to protect her from financial disaster?"

The bedrock of making the more prudent choice, to keep your client and try to put a lid on excessively large withdrawals that could mean financial abuse, is to have a third party to contact.

Many advisors already have this on file, but even more advisors focus only on the client, not on the family. Regulators do not yet require that you get that important third-party contact before you open an account. Neither do they require that you obtain third-party contact information at portfolio review on at least an annual basis for your senior clients. Without this information, and your client's permission to use it, you have nothing to go on when your client declines. This creates a serious problem when the telltale signs of cognitive decline creep up. What are you going to do with your client to ensure that they are not preyed upon by those who can't wait to get them to part with their money?

You can be left with no account at all for clients who are financially decimated by thieves. Their numbers are increasing. With an aging population, professional thieves are popping up everywhere: on the Internet, at the front door, in the elder's family, in caregiver disguise or in professional offices.

Research into financial elder abuse tells us several important things that apply to everyone who has an elder for a client. First, the most common abusers are family members. Have you seen this before?

**A Common Kind of Abuse—The Family Member**

A classic scenario is the elderly widow, unsophisticated about finances, whose husband used to make all the money decisions. The two of them appointed their son, qualified or not, to be the agent on the DPOA and to be the successor trustee with the widow or in her place. She has a large amount invested when she becomes a widow.

The son is not an honest person. He needs money, and he manipulates his mother easily. Cash disappears from her account. Sometimes he spends it down to zero, if drugs, alcohol, gambling or bad business decisions are part of the picture. He takes advantage and often gets away with it. Matters like this classic scene are rarely reported to authorities. Aging parents, fearing getting an adult child in trouble with the law, will not report or testify against the son.

**The Concept of Undue Influence**
Generally, the concept means using one's position of trust to manipulate another for the manipulator's good and not for the benefit of the elder. The obvious reason family members are the most frequent abusers of their elders is because of the relationship of trust. Abusers who seek out elders with the intention of taking advantage of them, such as telephone scammers, often work hard to establish trust before moving in for the request of the credit card or check.

In some states this idea of undue influence is defined by law. In other states it is not. That leads to uneven prosecution of financial elder abuse generated by undue influence across our country.

**What can the advisor do when a family member is taking advantage of your client?**
Sometimes your involvement can bring the abuse to a halt. For example, if another third party besides the suspicious adult child is identified in your client's file, you need to contact that person as soon as you are aware of a sign like unusually large withdrawals from your client's account. Just shining a light on an abuser can be enough to discourage or stop further predatory actions. In the example we offered in the last chapter about

Rhonda, whose mother was giving excessively larger and larger amounts to a charitable organization, the abuse stopped as soon as we suggested a meeting to discuss the matter with the organization and Rhonda.

Calling out the abuser doesn't always stop the abuse, but it certainly does work some of the time. And, at other times, when you have taken all reasonable steps to end abuse, your efforts may be in vain. Abuse is a persistent problem in families. When the victim of manipulation is a parent, that parent may be aware of the abuse and becomes essentially a willing victim.

According to the National Center on Elder Abuse, as few as 44 in 1,000 cases of financial elder abuse by a family member are reported to authorities.

"All too often, elderly victims are ashamed with being taken advantage of by someone close to them, a child even, or they don't want to see a relative get into legal trouble. They would rather suffer impoverishment than be the one to report the abuse," said Rhode Island Attorney General Kilmartin. "It is critically important for all those who are involved with caring for a senior—either financially or physically, and whether in a familial or professional relationship—to know the signs of abuse and to report it to the appropriate authorities. We owe our seniors at least that."

**Other Kinds of Financial Abuse**

Elders who use the Internet make desirable targets of professional thieves. The retired senior may have more hours to spend on the Internet than a younger employed person, and the predators know it. They seek out victims by various means, sometimes able to find them by age, desirable location or other indicators that there is something to steal. They are invariably friendly and work at establishing relationships with the seniors. And seniors who are also friendly are victimized more often than those who are less so, according to the True Link study mentioned above. Families can feel helpless in trying to stop an aging parent from involvement in an Internet relationship in which the elder becomes dependent and addicted.

**Illustration**

Christy and her brother were desperate when they called me. "What can we do?" she asked anxiously. "My dad lives alone in the country on a ranch. He's lonely since my mom passed. He got involved with this African rescue organization. We found out when I was looking at his email. They email him multiple times a day. I found out that over the last three years he has given them over $400,000!"

Christy had tried to talk to her father and told him there was no such legitimate organization. He was expecting a big reward for donating to them, being the biggest donor, he told her. She and her brother both argued with him about it. He told them they just didn't understand. He kept in contact with the predators.

My advice was to get financial control by using their power of attorney authority, which they finally did, along with getting their father to resign from the family trust and family business. Otherwise, he endangered the family's assets and business account from which he could draw cash. They had known that they needed to take action, but Christy and her brother were afraid their father would get angry with them if they insisted on using the DPOA.

Finally, with encouragement, they did take over. It took several months to stop the drain on their father's assets, as numerous meetings and the family business accountant were involved. Time often works against the elder. Illness or disability could rob him of his capacity to make decisions altogether, and each passing month can increase the risk of these factors. Time is on the side of the abuser, who may sense that there is only so long to squeeze as much out of a susceptible person as he can. He steps up the pressure to get more and often succeeds.

## What Could the Advisor Have Done?

Uncharacteristically large withdrawals had been draining out of the dad's account over a three-year period. Perhaps the advisor ignored this 86-year-old client's activity. In any case, he never contacted the family. Both Christy and her brother were appointed on their father's DPOA and should have been notified sooner.

In a properly structured senior program, the large withdrawals would have triggered the advisor to take protective action by contacting Christy and her brother. They had the power to put a stop to the fraud, but they didn't know about what their father was doing. He was addicted to the daily, incessant emails from the fraudulent organization, pretending to be racking up a big reward in the future for the dad.

*The advisor should have questioned his client about where the funds were going.* An 86-year-old living alone in the country probably was not spending $400,000 on his daily needs over the three years. It should have sounded an alarm to anyone managing the father's account. Further, the advisor, suspecting abuse, could have reported it to authorities.

## Is It a Violation of Your Client's Privacy Rights if You Report Financial Elder Abuse?

The short answer is "no."

All relevant federal agencies have issued interagency guidance on this issue. You do not have to search for and read their detailed explanation, as we are summarizing it, and simplifying it, for you right here. Their guidance document[16] has a single purpose: It is to help you understand that the Gramm-Leach-Bliley Act (GLBA), which sets out privacy requirements, does not preclude you from sharing otherwise private financial information about your clients when abuse is suspected. These agencies want you to report abuse!

You do not have to comply with notice and opt-out requirements that would otherwise apply to sharing of your client's private financial information.

Any financial professional would have to share such information if you got a subpoena from a lawsuit about it, or if your state or federal laws required you to disclose it to authorities. **You are also permitted to disclose this information to protect against or prevent actual or potential fraud**, unauthorized transactions, claims or other liability. You could also report financial abuse at the request of a client's legal representative. Be clear that the legal representative can either be a lawyer, or it can be the person appointed by the client as his agent (also called "attorney in fact") on a durable power of attorney document.

In the illustration about Christy, above, the advisor could have contacted authorities, even if the family did not do so. One needs a reasonable belief that fraud or abuse is occurring. You do not have to have absolute proof or be totally sure. A reasonable belief could be gained from learning that the elder's addiction to a suspicious charity had resulted in his gift to them of $400,000 and that this was completely out of character, as the advisor knew him over a number of years.

---

[16] Interagency Guidance on Privacy Laws and Reporting Financial Abuse of Older Persons, Board of Governors of the Federal Reserve System, Commodity Futures Trading Commission, Consumer Financial Protection Bureau, Federal Deposit Insurance Corporation, Federal Trade Commission, National Credit Union Administration, Office of the Comptroller of the Currency and Securities Exchange Commission. https://www.fdic.gov/news/news/press/2013/Interagency-Guidance-on-Privacy-Laws-and-Reporting-Financial-Abuse-of-Older-Adults.pdf?source=govdelivery. (last accessed 5.12.16)

New model rules that regulators are developing even as we write this book will add some clear protections for you when you report elder abuse. Under those rules you would receive a "safe harbor," which means that you could not be sued for reporting financial abuse, even if you were mistaken in what you thought was abuse. A similar protection already exists for those who are now mandated to report financial abuse: physicians, nurses, health care workers, home care helpers, licensed fiduciaries and the like. State laws determine who must report abuse, and those laws vary from state to state.

### The Warning Signs

Warning signs of elder financial abuse are many, as abuse can take many forms. It can come from family, as described, from caregivers, from professionals and from thieves who seek out vulnerable elders by telephone or the Internet. It can be helpful to you, with greater protection of your senior investors in mind, to recognize some of the common warning signs.

### Seven Warning Signs May Include the Following

**1.** Your client has always had a trusted person whom, some time ago, he appointed as an agent on his durable power of attorney form. **Suddenly he changes and gives the DPOA power to a different person**, and you question that new person's motives and behavior.

**2.** Your client, whom you've known for some time, is **not able to access her own funds** under your management, as well as other financial assets and property. Her assets appear to be under the control of someone else, who has stopped your client from making any decisions about her money.

## SUCCEED WITH SENIOR CLIENTS

3. You receive **a change of address notice,** indicating that your client is no longer receiving mail at the location where he has been for as long as you've known him. You heard nothing from him about moving and were sure he did not want to move. You question this change of address.

**4. Isolation**
When you call your client, someone else answers the phone and says your client is out or otherwise unavailable. Your written communication attempts to contact your client receive no response. After many tries, you get the impression that someone is stopping your client from taking your calls.

**5. Odd change in investment choices**
Your client has always been a conservative investor, preferring low-risk products over the long period of time you've known him. Suddenly he wants to withdraw cash to put into things you consider very high risk, if not downright dangerous.

6. In checking your client's account, you notice numerous **large withdrawals, unexplained** and completely outside the norm for your client.

**7. Appearance of a new "friend"**
Your client comes to your office with a relative or friend whom you have never met and who has never before been involved in your client's financial matters. Your client seems pressured to include this other individual in obtaining all of his account information and to direct transactions.

In all of these warning signs, there is a departure from what has previously been normal for your clients. Be particularly conscious that family members, supposedly the most trusted, are the most frequent abusers. Find out about the relationship your client has with an adult child or grandchild. Is that person in need of money, and is he doing questionable things, like manipulating your client into taking out cash and giving it to this relative?

Should you get into your client's personal business and ask what might be considered "nosy" questions? We say "yes," you should. Elder abuse is everyone's business. If financial professionals do not get more involved in spotting the problem and reporting it, then it will only grow. Few elders themselves report abuse. Shame and embarrassment are too often attached to the experience of being financially abused, and these emotions prevent reporting the crime. Thieves continue to get away with it.

**Caregiver Abuse**

Your client may need some help at home as she ages. She may need to go to assisted living or another kind of care facility. Particularly while your client is able to remain at home, as most people prefer, a home care provider is the usual choice. There are issues with the entire process of hiring home care workers. Many elders find workers on recommendations from friends or neighbors, and it can work well to do the hiring that way. However, there are hidden dangers for your client.

A vulnerable older person, particularly with memory loss, is unlikely to be sophisticated in hiring help to work at home. Unscrupulous home care workers are alone and unsupervised with an elder for many hours each time they visit. They may be going to the grocery store or other places where they handle the client's money. Some accompany the client to the bank. When a worker is desperate because of her own life circumstances, the temptation to steal from your client may be too much to resist. Stealing from a person with memory loss who depends on a care worker is easy. If they are privately hired, they answer to no one other than the elder. Even if they are hired through an agency, which we recommend as the best choice, the risk remains if the worker needs money.

**Illustration**

Jerry is 90, physically infirm and is in the early stages of Alzheimer's disease. He lives with his wife in a comfortable home in an expensive county. She has gotten various kinds of help for him as his health declined and eventually hired a worker from an agency. The worker came several times a week to take Jerry out to lunch, to his pool exercises and to the bank. Jerry took out $1,000 at a time in cash from the bank, which the caregiver observed. He used it for his lunches and just for fun things he enjoyed doing.

He kept the cash in his clothes drawer, which the caregiver knew, as she often helped him get dressed in the morning.

One day the $1,000 was missing. Jerry asked his wife if she had taken it. No, she hadn't. Did he forget where he put it? Maybe. But after a search, the conclusion was that the only person who had access to the cash other than Jerry himself was the caregiver. Jerry's wife reported it immediately to the agency that supplied the caregiver. They would not admit the theft. But Jerry's wife fired the agency and got a different caregiver. This time around there were no more cash transactions involving caregivers.

Imagine that Jerry was alone and completely dependent on the caregiver. Imagine that the agency or the caregiver herself denied taking the cash and blamed Jerry for forgetting where he had put the money. Imagine that the caregiver used her relationship with Jerry to manipulate him into giving her money. All of these scenarios are common and are the reason we count caregivers as the second most common abusers of seniors next to family members.

## Desperation and Opportunity

The caregiver was beloved by Jerry, which was a relationship that became dangerous. She probably figured he would not suspect her. The caregiver had revealed to Jerry's wife the week of the theft that her husband had left her and that she had two children at home. Desperation had driven her to steal, somehow believing that she would get away with it. And it was easy. She knew where the cash was, and she also knew that Jerry easily forgot things.

This is not at all atypical. Thefts like this are common and seldom reported to authorities. Jerry's wife did not want to report the caregiver because her husband had left her and she had two small children. The case was not formally resolved. It ended when Jerry's wife refused to pay the final caregiver agency bill, which was about the same amount as the missing cash. The agency did not pursue it.

## Stakes Can Be High

In one case, unfortunately not an atypical case, a caregiver for a 74-year-old disabled woman stole everything the woman had in assets. Real estate and investments, worth $4 million, were sucked away over six years. The caregiver was living a grand life, putting her son through an expensive private college, driving new cars and gambling. She had 62 accounts in ten banks where she used her client's funds. One of the banks finally got suspicious, but it was very late in the game. With that much in assets, we question where her financial advisor was during the hemorrhaging of everything she owned?

Many of the signs of financial abuse would have been present.

Isolation, change of address for financial statements, the caregiver showing up at the bank repeatedly and uncharacteristically large withdrawals were just a few of the things that should have sounded the alarm something was not right.

The caregiver and her son were charged with the crime of financial elder abuse, convicted and did serve time in jail. The elder died before they served their sentences.

**What Does This Mean for You?**
We suggest that you not be blind to the risks to your aging clients in having caregivers at home. The regulators want you to educate your clients about known risks to seniors. Theft by caregivers is one of them. Here are three things you can do when you learn that your client is going to need help at home and is going to have a caregiver. You may be increasing your client's drawdown from her funds to pay for the increased expense. Help your client out with a few cautionary instructions. You could save her from a lot of trouble. The tips on best ways to choose a home care worker are spelled out more fully in another book that may be useful for client education.[17] (This is Available at AgingParents.com.)

**1. Encourage them to use a licensed agency to supply the worker**. The desire to save money by hiring from the Internet or from recommendations may not be worth the risk. Not all agencies are created equal, and theft can occur even with an agency-supplied worker, but agencies are typically insured, and hiring involves a background check. Yes, it is more expensive to hire through an agency. But at least some supervision occurs when

---

[17] Carolyn Rosenblatt, "How to Choose A Home Care Worker" in The Family Guide to Aging Parents, Answers to Your Legal, Financial and Healthcare Questions, (Familius, 2015), 195-220. Healthcare Questions, (Familius, 2015), 195-220.

the worker is the agency's employee. That eliminates some risk factors for your client.

**2. Encourage them and their family members to remove temptation,** in the form of expensive objects and jewelry, from easy access by any home care worker. Help them to recognize that temptation can become too much for a relatively low-earning home care worker in your client's expensive environment. Valuable, portable objects can easily be pocketed or taken by caregivers, and no one notices.

**3. Educate your client to never allow a home care worker to have access** to cash, bank accounts or to conduct financial transactions for an aging client. Most normal purchases can be done electronically by a fully competent person other than your client to avoid the use of cash by the worker. One conscientious home care agency we know uses gift or debit cards in limited amounts for all its home care workers, and the boss tracks the amounts spent on a daily basis via an electronic record on his computer. He then bills the client each month for the debit card the worker uses. It works very well. No thefts with his agency.

**Telephone Scams, Internet Thieves and "Front Door Fraud"**
Another aspect of financial abuse that many public agencies try to warn about is fraud from those who target seniors specifically. These fraudsters may be rings of professional criminals who make millions doing this, or it may be some other low-life opportunists who know where to find elderly folks. Some knock on doors offering home repairs, and then take the money and run without doing the work. Others buy names of seniors and dial for dollars until they find a mark.

This is where your efforts to warn and educate your clients

can join the efforts of local law enforcement, the National Center on Elder Abuse (NCEA) and the American Association of Retired Persons (AARP), as well as local senior centers. All of the public agencies have available educational materials you can download and print for the benefit of your older clients. All of them provide tips and information about how to prevent being scammed.

Despite all these efforts, older people may be caught at a vulnerable moment or may be just impaired enough that they do not see a scam coming. Billions of dollars are being lost every year from a combination of ways. Telephone and Internet scammers continue to succeed in stealing. The best you can do is try to alert your own clients so they do not fall victim to these clever thieves. Your efforts to help them, understanding not to give out credit card or Social Security numbers to anyone who calls them, can save a client from a scam. Since the subject of preventing elder abuse is one of the regulators' confirmed areas of interest and recommendations, we suggest you take their advice. One way to do that is to create a basic, straightforward information resource about elder abuse prevention for your aging clients. It should be part of your senior-focused new program we advocate that you initiate in your office or firm.

All of the material you need is already created, available to you through NCEA, AARP or other government sites. You can put a resource page on your website with links to the booklets or information sheets, or you can print them and send or give them to your clients. When you do this, you are showing not only the regulators that you get their message, but you are also showing your clients that you are concerned for their financial safety. Your relationship and image cannot be harmed, and will likely be enhanced, if you put that message forth to your clients.

## Professional Financial Abuse

Professionals in your client's life can become thieves, too. Sadly enough, professionals know how much a client has and how to get control over it. Some have unfettered discretion over client funds. In some cases they can steal without being detected. These professionals include lawyers, guardians, real estate brokers and, yes, financial professionals, among others.

The issue of unsuitable investments sold to elders is one part of this abuse. That is something the regulators are very interested in stopping. We are looking at the larger problem of not only inappropriate sales of financial products to vulnerable seniors but also of the issue of undue influence by financial professionals to get clients to go along with suggestions they should never make to seniors.

## The Solution to Abuse in Your Profession

We see two clear ways to prevent financial abuse of clients your organization serves. These are **increased frequency of account reviews and a higher degree of supervision than that normally given** over accounts of younger clients. That closer supervision includes surveillance. Both of these means are suggestions the regulators have already set out in their writings. They want you to do things differently for older clients than you normally do with younger clients. They are looking closely at the "culture" of firms, to determine whether the sale of questionable or unsuitable products is tolerated or not. The firm's culture may include a general attitude that no special attention need be paid to older investors. That can get you in trouble if it manifests as actions that regulators prosecute: e.g., sale of disproportionate percentages of variable annuities in a senior's portfolio or sale of non-traded REITs to people of advanced age.

## Illustration

This is a case much too close to home. It involved my mother-in-law, Alice, Dr. Davis' own mom, age 90 at the time. Her trusted advisor sold her a non-traded REIT (real estate investment trust), which she never understood was going to tie up her funds for 12 years or more. She grew disenchanted with her advisor, who was not growing her portfolio, and she chose to change advisors. Her decision was not based on the REIT. It was based on seeing a year-end statement showing portfolio growth of 1%, while knowing the advisor's fee was 1%. She simply wanted to see a little growth, and he had not performed well. At the time her funds were being transferred out to someone else she chose to manage her money, she learned that the money in the REIT could not be accessed. She was very upset!

## Our Shock

Dr. Davis and I are deeply involved in education for financial professionals to prevent or stop elder abuse, and in this case abuse had happened right under our noses. Dr. Davis reviews his mother's accounts monthly. Nothing in the paperwork informed him of the nature of the investment in the REIT such that it made funds inaccessible. The broker who had sold this investment to Alice was immediately confronted. He had a lot of excuses, of course. She made the investment "for the benefit of her heirs" was one of them. When Alice was asked about this, she vehemently denied making any investments for that purpose. "I have to take care of myself first," she said. Dr. Davis was appointed as the agent on Alice's durable power of attorney. Still, they delayed and delayed at the advisor's office in providing information to him when requested.

Several telephone conversations, lawyer involvement for the broker-dealer and an ultimatum to rescind the sale or get reported to FINRA and the SEC resulted in a refund of the invested funds to Alice. All of this occurred before the Department of Labor fiduciary rule had become law. We expect things would have been even worse for the B-D if that standard were in place when he sold Alice that REIT.

Now, imagine if the B-D involved were your colleague. Who was supervising him? Regulators had been prosecuting firms for selling non-traded REITs to seniors, and firms had been paying large fines for the practice at the time the sale took place. If you saw the sale of a non-traded REIT to a 90-year-old in your office, would anyone else be aware of it? Would the action be reviewed if it took place this week?

This is precisely the sort of thing regulators have in mind when they recommend surveillance, enhanced reviews and closer supervision over aging investors' accounts. If you want to stay clear of prosecutions and fines, look in your own backyard for any unscrupulous characters among you. It happens in some of the best firms. One bad apple can embarrass the ethical people in an organization, causing regulators to question why the organization did not monitor and supervise that bad apple more effectively. Close monitoring of aging investors' accounts is one way to thwart the unsavory activities that get firms in trouble. We interviewed Alice about this purchase of the REIT, which, of course, she never did understand. The interview is posted on YouTube, with the name and organization of the B-D kept confidential. View it here: **https://www.youtube.com/watch?v=sgvIGe673JQ**

## How Often Should Aging Clients' Accounts Be Reviewed?

The regulators do not set out any exact formula for stepped-up frequency of aging client portfolio reviews. However, if you review all portfolios annually, you obviously have to go over aging clients' accounts more often than that. Twice a year may be enough. However, if your client has demonstrated signs of diminished capacity, twice a year may not be sufficient. Your senior program should include a plan as to how often your office will review aging client accounts.

It should also include a provision to review, on an even more frequent basis, the accounts of clients who have been identified as having diminished capacity than those older clients whose cognition seems fine. If a client is showing signs of memory loss and is borderline, in your opinion, in being able to make safe financial decisions, it is prudent to review the portfolio quarterly and/or to determine that her capacity for financial decision is a question, and it should be escalated to find the next steps.

## SUMMARY

Financial elder abuse in the U.S. is a $36-billion-a-year problem. The role of the advisor can be instrumental in stopping it, or preventing it, altogether. The regulators want you to take an active role in paying attention to aging clients' needs in a different way from how you look at other clients' accounts.

Know the seven warning signs of elder abuse. If you see them, you can report your suspicions to authorities, or you may be able to involve a trusted third party, perhaps a family member. Regulators do not want you to ignore the issue and "just manage the money." They want your job to be bigger than that. They may give you a rule that says you can hold transactions for a short time once you have identified abuse, but you are expected to know what to do within that time frame.

You can educate your own clients about the risks of elder financial abuse. You can call it to the attention of anyone who could intervene. This includes those in your own profession who could be involved in unapproved sales of inappropriate products to seniors. If you are in an organization, create enhanced supervision, monitoring and surveillance over aging investors' accounts. Review all older clients' accounts at least twice a year.

**Appendix 2** to this book gives you this summary of the 7 Warning Signs of Abuse in checklist form. Feel free to copy it, pass it around and adopt it in your office in any form. No time for that? Here's the essence of the checklist, just to remind you once more. Watch for:

**1. Sudden change in the assigned DPOA power to a different person**, and you question that new person's motives and behavior.

**2. Your client is not able to access her own funds,** under your management.

**3. You receive a change of address notice**, and you question this unexplained change of address.

**4. Isolation**
**You can't reach your client.** Someone is stopping your client from taking your calls.

**5.** Odd **change in investment choices**. Your client suddenly wants to invest in things you consider very high risk.

**6. Numerous large withdrawals, unexplained** and completely outside the norm for your client.

**7. Appearance of a new "friend."** Your client comes to your office with a relative or friend whom you have never met and who has never before been involved in your client's financial matters.

# 4

# TOUGH TALK: COMMUNICATION CHALLENGES WITH AGING CLIENTS

**INTRODUCTION**
We hope you feel that you communicate well with every client in your book of business. But, as people age, there may be increasing difficulty in ordinary communication for a number of age-related reasons. Obstacles exist. In this chapter we explore some of the obstacles you will encounter and address how to overcome them. Above all, your awareness of possible problems can raise your level of planning and your readiness to meet these communication challenges. Older clients have both physical and cognitive changes that must shape the way you communicate with them.

**What's Different About Older Clients?**
As we spelled out earlier in this book, we have to anticipate that some elders are going to develop cognitive decline as they age. This precipitates the need to involve third parties. If you're smart, you've already identified who should be contacted if your client's ability to make good financial decisions begins to fade. But getting your client's permission to make that contact may not be so easy.

## SUCCEED WITH SENIOR CLIENTS

**A Problem: Secrecy About Finances**

For your clients who are now in their 80s, 90s and beyond, the experience of living in the U.S. through the Great Depression shaped their attitudes and beliefs about money. Some have felt that they would never have enough money throughout their lives. Others, having been deprived of so much when they were young, become reckless spenders later on, and they cannot see a need to be prudent in their spending, even as their long life drains the amounts in reserve. They have trouble acknowledging the need to pay for late life expenses, such as costly long-term care.

A consistent communication challenge we see in our work is the resistance of the older person to discuss finances with anyone, including their adult children or other heirs. The Great Depression led to secrecy about finances for many, as fortunes were lost sometimes overnight, and once-proud people became impoverished. Talking openly about money was just not done for those who grew up in this time of widespread devastating and, sometimes, life-ending financial losses. To this segment of our population, openly discussing money was considered rude, unseemly. Some of these Depression-era survivors remain reluctant to tell anyone in their families where their accounts are, what their assets are and what they want done with their assets in the event of incapacity.

**How Secrecy Can Cause You to Lose Clients**

Nothing sets a person up for abuse more than developing cognitive impairment, refusing to share any financial information and isolating himself from others who would have to step in to help. You, the financial professional, eventually have to ask your client for permission to do things with the portfolio. If he cannot make or appreciate the need for a decision, you cannot act. The matter may then be escalated to compliance. If it is determined that your client is no longer competent, you are precluded from contacting a third party, and that is the dead end. Compliance will likely advise that your client is now a liability to the firm or organization. The answer is to get rid of the client. We think there are other, more forward-thinking, options. You do not have to lose every client who becomes impaired.

## A Solution: Use the Power of Your Relationship

Your secretive client may be fearful that if family or heirs know what the elder has, that they will take advantage of her. Or she may be uncomfortable sharing information because "it's none of their business" to know what she has in the way of assets you manage. But it is clear from the other parts of this book addressing elder abuse and diminished capacity that someone has to be empowered to step in and stand in your client's shoes if she is to be protected from dangerous decisions or financial fraud and abuse. Presumably, when you have a long-term relationship with your client, she trusts you and trusts your judgment. That gives you leverage. You may know more about her finances than her family, her friends or anyone in her life. You are charged with the task of long-range planning and you look ahead. In doing so, it is up to you to urge your client, gently, repeatedly and with ongoing persistence, that she find someone she can trust to appoint to protect her if she has an accident, falls ill or can't speak for herself.

You may be unaccustomed to "getting into your client's personal life," but you have no real choice here. Clients grow old, they develop problems in thinking, and you cannot pretend that everything is fine. Since some clients are going to live to be 100 and more these days, you definitely need a plan as to how you will address the aging issues and the secrecy that may have been your client's habit for a long time, maybe a lifetime.

If you prefer to let the situation with an aging client who has cognitive impairment decline to the point of no return, you can make that choice. You are likely to lose that client, because things are going to go wrong sooner or later. If you want to retain the client, consider how to do it.

## Sometimes Persistence Pays

You need to bring up the subject of your client's future needs and possible incapacity tactfully and gently. You can mention that a client who lives to be "old" (they never think this applies to *them*) must plan ahead for the possibility of needing someone to speak for them. We suggest that you never bring up the subject of dementia or cognitive impairment as something that might happen. People are not only terrified at the thought and often in denial that it could ever happen to them, but they can't relate to this kind of warning. Instead, use the more familiar "in case of emergency," or "what if you were in an accident and could not talk" question, to broach the subject. This is a decidedly less threatening approach. If your client resists, make note, document as you normally would and try again. Keep repeating your concern. You may break through.

## The Risk of Waiting Too Long

There is no question that talking about accidents, disability and the possible need for someone else having to know your client's personal financial affairs is uncomfortable. It might be more uncomfortable for you than it is for your client.

Whatever the reason, be it client resistance or your own hesitation to delve into something outside your own comfort zone, we caution you to set a date and have the conversation. If you wait until your client becomes impaired, you are taking two major risks.

## The Risk of Guardianship or Conservatorship

First, if your client does not have the capacity any longer to appoint someone on a power of attorney document, no one can legally handle the client's affairs for him without going to court. A judge can appoint a guardian or conservator, but this is expensive, time-consuming and can be very embarrassing to your client. Unless the client is severely impaired and unable to communicate at all, cognitive impairment does not erase the ability to experience emotions, such as shame and embarrassment. If you can avoid having a client dragged into court to listen to how bad his memory is or what a mess things are for him, that is certainly better for the client. And there is also the possibility that a stranger could be appointed by the court to handle the client's affairs if no family or close person has been appointed by your client. The court-appointed conservator or guardian may not want you to continue to manage the client's portfolio and will move it elsewhere. There go your fees for management of that portfolio.

## The Risk of Dangerous Financial Decisions

In our work we have seen a second risk appear repeatedly. Imagine yourself with a longtime client who seems to be "losing it." He has no power of attorney and doesn't want to talk about it. He says, "It's my money, and I'll do what I want with it." He doesn't trust his own family.

The elder is experiencing a slow but steady cognitive decline. No one acts. No one insists that the client choose a relative or friend to be the agent on the durable power of attorney document. He says he doesn't want to talk about it, and you just back off and never mention it again.

The client steadily loses judgment about what is a good thing to spend money on or invest in; therefore, bad decisions happen. We have observed clients, who were once financially comfortable, start falling for obvious scams. They buy worthless coins or stamps or fly-by-night property investments that take their money and disappear. Perhaps no one knows, because the elder is in the secrecy habit. Time passes, and the client's cognitive ability declines even more. There is no stopping dementia caused by Alzheimer's disease. The predators find an easy mark. As long as there is cash to spend or credit cards to run up, the elder keeps getting into deeper and deeper trouble. Unquestionably, financial decimation can result.

These situations are real. We have talked to the families of elders who have probably been impaired for years, hearing them say they wished someone had done something sooner. No one but the financial professional knew what the client had or where his money was going. The family thought the elder's finances were fine. Now, with too much drained out by scammers, con artists and thieves, the family may well end up having to support their aging relative just at the time when extensive care is needed and the expense of it skyrockets.

## Why Should You Get Involved?

The regulators want you to do something other than sit by and watch your client commit financial suicide. "It's his money, and he can do what he wants with it" is a very limited view. To us it is also cold-hearted. What your client wants may not be tempered by intact judgment. People with good judgment do not want to end up in poverty when they have another choice. If you can keep him safer by using the power of your relationship to rein him in and get someone else involved in his financial life, the effort is worth it. Urging your client, by patient repetition, to open up the discussion about the portfolio not only protects him but also protects you from losing the client and his invested funds.

We address the privacy issue in detail in Chapter 3. We hope you see from that that you need not fear breaking privacy rules because there is a work-around solution in a special privacy document. Your client can give you permission in such a specially drafted document to contact a third party. Permission can also be verbal, on the spot, in a discussion, to include a family member, friend or trusted other in the converation. The gist of our suggestions is that you should ask for your client's permission to contact a third party if the need arises. And remind your client that the need to do so is likely as we age. This applies to everyone, not just a particular client.

Anticipating possible diminished capacity ahead of time is the very thing that may enable you to retain the client you don't want to lose. Protecting your client is the same mechanism you undertake to protect your fees. With an impaired client you will need that third-party involvement.

Clearly you cannot talk every client into doing the smart thing, and the safe thing, and discussing finances with a trusted other. Some stubborn folks will refuse any good advice in this regard. You may end up losing those clients anyway, as the course of cognitive impairment will ultimately end in a kind of mental collapse for the client if he lives long enough. For the rest of your clients who may be inclined to listen to you because they trust you, use that trust to help them help themselves with this secrecy problem. It is just too dangerous to ignore. Ignoring the issue, or letting him do anything he wants with his funds, regardless of obviously declining ability to understand his finances, just puts that client at greater risk of financial abuse.

## Why Is This Your Problem and Not Just the Family's?

As we hope you can see by what we have discussed to this point, looking out for your aging clients starts with wanting to do the right things for them. Ultimately it may be driven by your desire to keep assets under management. Your motivation is not as important as the action you take. You are in a unique role. You know your client, and may know her better than her family and friends. You have, in many cases, an opportunity to keep her on the right track with planning for aging in a way even family cannot. Getting the conversation about finances going, and appointing the right successor and decision-maker, will undoubtedly help your client if she becomes impaired. That appointed person stands in the shoes of your client for decision-making, working with you to meet the client's known goals for investing.

Of course, for clients who have family, there is also a responsibility the family has to mind their elders and step up when they see impairment. But some families do not get along. Some are in denial about an aging parent's cognition. And some elders refuse to talk to family about finances unless someone they trust keeps bringing it up. Your power of persuasion depends on your relationship of trust.

**Other Communication Issues With Aging Clients**
**Memory Loss**
As we described earlier in this book, from the first two chapters, memory loss with aging is common and often is the first sign of dementia developing in your client. When your client calls you repeatedly in the same day, forgetting an earlier conversation you've already had, you may think this client is going downhill a bit but it's probably okay. And you may think you'll worry about it later or you'll wait "until something happens." That is likely the most typical reaction financial professionals have: worry about the memory loss later. But when you see memory loss, *something is already happening.* This is certainly a communication issue for you. You don't know if the client remembers your

advice, or even remembers why she called you. We suggest that the best way to address memory loss in your older client is to first document it and then set a date to follow up with another conversation to test whether the memory problem is consistent. This is a client who needs your observation **within a month of the first signs of memory loss**. If a transaction needs to take place, and your client gives you the necessary approval, that is not the problem. It is what happens the next time, or the next month, or even the following year. The nature of cognitive impairment is that it often happens gradually, and your client may be very inconsistent in how she presents. You may think, when she can't recall that you already answered her question or can't remember that you asked her for a decision, that she's just having a bad day. However, she may be gradually losing her grasp of what you are telling her or asking her.

**What You Should Do**
If you are unsure of the extent of your client's memory issue, **contact your client again within a month of when you first noticed memory loss** and find out if she remembers your prior discussion or a transaction you talked about. Or you can ask her about a point you made and see if she recalls it a few days or weeks later. The kind of memory loss that indicates possible dementia is **short-term memory loss**. Your client may be able to tell you in great and accurate detail what happened 50 years ago. But if she can't recall what happened last week or yesterday, that puts you on notice of a potential problem that needs your follow-up.

Document your observations. Keep enough of a record that you are reasonably sure that this is a pattern over time. If he keeps forgetting things, your documentation will reveal how many times this has happened within the framework of your observations and notes about them. When you have a record to work from, you now have something to rely on when you approach your client with the problem. Ask your client to meet with you. In person is the best, but Skype™ or telephone will have to do if your client is far away.

**What You Should Say to Your Client**
There are words that work in difficult conversations and words that don't work. Making your client wrong, naming what you think might be dementia, or other strong words, are not a good choice. Using tact, and starting with your own perception, is safer.

**We offer you some sample scripts and video demonstrations in our online course, *Best Practices For Communication Challenges With Aging Investors*.**[18] **For more information, go to www.AgingInvestor.com/courses**.

In the course we describe how to first approach the client with what YOU are worried about, not what is wrong with her. For example, you would say the following.

"Mary, I've noticed that you seem to be forgetting what we talked about early in the day, and you asked me about it again later when you called back the same day. That has me concerned."

Expect some pushback from your client. Most people get defensive when you point out that you have a concern about their thinking powers. But this is where you use your documentation. No matter what your client says in response, do not argue with her. Simply show her that you have notes of your conversations, and that you now have six instances, or whatever the number of calls, asking you to repeat something you discussed earlier that day or week.

---

[18] AgingInvestor.com, online CFP Board approved one hour course *Best Practices For Communication Challenges With Aging Investors.* (last accessed May 8, 2016)

# SUCCEED WITH SENIOR CLIENTS

Explain why you are worried, as this could mean that she could forget something very important for her finances and that you want to involve that third party you and she had wisely planned for a long time ago.

Another tactic that generally works well is to point out to your client that if she does not share any financial information with her adult children or appointee, she will become a burden. Most parents do not want to see themselves as a burden to their children or other family. And those who do not have children do not want to become a burden to their friends. Paint a scenario for her. Ask her to imagine being in an accident and being unable to speak afterward, such as being in a coma. Ask her who would have authority to sign a check for her, or who would pay the bills when she was in a hospital. How would this person know what she has and how to pay for the care she could require?

When you have to bring up these delicate personal things, it will not be easy, but it must be done. Perhaps the stumbling block that prevents financial professionals from bringing up these concerns with clients is the discomfort it entails. Here's a scenario that may help you overcome that uncomfortable feeling.

**Illustration**

Imagine your client, a widow, age 89, with a portfolio of $4 million. Now imagine that she begins to lose her memory before your eyes but you say nothing. She feels magnanimous and makes large donations to her favorite charity. She forgets that she has already written a check for the usual amount and writes another one a month later. The charity loves it and keeps sending more solicitations. Friends and family ask her for money, and she cheerfully gives away more and more of it. She can't remember what is in her portfolio, but she's sure everything is fine. She is wealthy, after all.

Her grandson has a gambling and drug habit. He keeps asking her for money and persuades her to get a mortgage on her home. She complies. Her house is now heavily encumbered. Her memory loss is steady but slow. Four years pass from the time you first noted forgetfulness. Each year the portfolio is smaller, and now it is down to $1 million. At the same time, your client has a stroke. She is now in a wheelchair and needs full-time care at home. She refuses to go into a nursing home or assisted living facility. She wants to remain in her own home. She is 92 when she has the stroke. Full-time care costs her over $200,000 a year. She lives to be 98. She has run out of money completely by age 95, with the cost of living and the cost of caregivers. She has to sell her home, and by the time the loan is paid off, she has enough for a care facility, which is something she said she never, ever, wanted to do. She spends her last days miserably, depressed that she is not in her beautiful home and must live in a facility. Is that what you worked for over the years, to see her end up this way?

The story is not far-fetched, and it can, and does, happen to plenty of elders who are otherwise financially secure. They lose their wealth near the end of life due to cognitive decline, abuse and the failure of those around them, including the financial advisor, to take action before it is too late. This is preventable. It requires the intervention of professionals, the financial advisor, among them. You may be the one to sound the alarm. You may be the one, with your prudent foresight, to involve a caring family member. You may be the one to stop the effects of your client's loss of judgment about what is safe to do with her money. Memory loss is not the only age-related issue you are likely to face in client communication. Age takes numerous kinds of physical tolls, of course, as the wear and tear of years of living emerges before you. The physical impairments your client may have should be part of your consciousness and planning as to how to ensure excellent communication with the client.

## Physical Impairments as Communication Challenges
### Hearing loss

Most of us probably know someone who is hard of hearing but refuses to wear a hearing aid. The greater the number of older clients you have, the more likely you are to find some with hearing loss. And it can be quite frustrating for the advisor trying to communicate with an aging client who can't hear you very well. According to the National Institutes of Health, there is a strong relationship between age and reported hearing loss: 18% of American adults 45-64 years old, 30% of adults 65-74 years old and 47% of adults 75 years old, or older, have a hearing impairment.[19] What is it that causes so many older people to refuse to wear a hearing aid? There are numerous reasons, including unwillingness to see the problem as others do. Here's one example.

My mother-in-law, Alice, now 93, would not get a hearing aid at age 90, even though she often had to ask others to repeat what they had just said. At one point I sat down with her and her two best friends. I asked Alice if she thought she ever missed any of the conversation others had with her because she didn't hear it. "Yes," she said. I asked her what percentage of conversations she thought she was missing. She estimated about 10%. I then asked her friends their opinion of how much of the conversations with them she missed when they spoke with her. They estimated about 50% or more. Apparently, that was enough to get Alice to the ear doctor to get her hearing loss evaluated. And she did get hearing aids. They are uncomfortable at times.

---

[19] http://nihseniorhealth.gov/hearingloss/hearinglossdefined/01.html. (last accessed May 16, 2016)

They itch. Sometimes the background noise is amplified when it should not be. The batteries do go out unexpectedly. But her pride and desire not to miss what others are saying was enough to motivate her. Prior to that it seemed Alice just didn't like the idea of hearing aids because that meant she was "old." A lot of other seniors are the same way. They don't want to identify as "old" and don't want to wear or use the devices that would make day-to-day life easier because of a fearful attitude about aging itself. Likewise, they sometimes refuse to look ahead at what longevity for them might entail. It would mean getting old.

**Our Ageist Society**
Older folks seem to spend a lot of time in denial of aging. They could be in their 90s, and see others as "old," but not themselves as such. In working with adult families we have often heard seniors tell us that they'll attend to that (planning for longevity, accepting the need for care, refusing to share financial information with their heirs, etc.) later. "I'll get to that when I'm old. I'm just not ready yet." Getting old is not valued in our society. Ageist attitudes are everywhere. Older people are often dismissed as having less importance than younger people. In this country we are a youth-oriented culture as much as we are a work-driven society. Look at what you see most often in the things that shape our attitudes: TV, movies, the Internet, news, magazines, music and, especially, advertising. Young images dominate. Enjoyment of life is often depicted through the prism of youth.

We tend to spend less time talking and thinking about the phase of life that involves aging and no longer being productive through work. Although a huge segment of our population is retired or retiring, we do not, as a general trend, focus on the positives that can characterize an aging person. Instead, the media, if focused at all on older subjects, is usually filled with images of unrealistic, fantasy-like retirement years, as if it were all fun vacation time. Even in the heavy advertising push to sell medications and devices of every kind to older people, media does not often address the dignity and beauty of wisdom that can accompany aging. No wonder older people try to avoid embracing their own aging. There is such negative programming about it for them. And the same negative programming can affect financial professionals working with older clients as well. We may dismiss aging as a topic, we may deny its impact in planning, and we may sidestep the accommodations needed in the way we communicate with clients as they age. In short, there is more to retirement planning than making money last. There are the risks of aging itself that need to be included in planning. Financial professionals must not let their own possibly negative attitudes about aging color what is discussed for retirement planning.

**The Solution**
If we want to get along well and communicate at an optimum with our older investors, we need to be conscious of our own need to **adapt to their age-related changes.** Take a moment to consider your client's age, what issues he or she might have, and make your adjustments. Observe when you see your client face to face. You can learn a lot if you are aware of the need to be more observant.

**What You Can Do With Hearing Loss**
When an older client comes into my office, I can either tell that he can't hear well early in the interaction, or a family member informs me "he's really hard of hearing," or "he won't get a hearing aid." So, when I need to speak to the elder, I **sit close**. I move

over if I need to ask him something. **I face him directly**. Many older people with hearing loss adjust to it by some lip-reading. They do this better when you are facing them. And remember that hearing aids are not a perfect solution. Not only are some kinds of hearing loss not fixable with hearing aids, but these devices are also not always working the way they should. Be kind. The struggle to hear can make your job harder, but patience and asking for feedback from your older client can be very helpful. It is perfectly okay to ask your client if he can hear you all right.

**What You Can Do About Your Pace**
Adapting to your client's age-related changes also involves **slowing down your pace** with some clients. Age can cause us to process information more slowly than when we were younger. If your client seems to take longer to "get it" when you explain something, try saying it more slowly. Ask if she understood you. Put it another way if the uptake seems slow for that client. This slower processing may not have anything to do with dementia or memory. It may have nothing to do with intelligence. It just might be that the work of taking in and understanding concepts moves at a different pace now. Aging clients will likely take more of your time when you need to review things, get permissions, explain your suggestions for changes to the portfolio. Patience is an excellent communication tool with aging clients. And we hope that is fine with you. After all, these elders are ourselves a few years down the road.

**What You Can Do About Accessibility**
Should you have a number of older investors in your book, be sure to attend to their needs in your environment. **Mobility may be a problem**. If you are in the kind of building that does not have an elevator, offer to go to your client rather than the other

way around, or offer to meet your client in an accessible place. It is your consciousness of these needs that communicates your understanding and appreciation for what your client needs, and your client is likely to appreciate it as well.

## What You Can Do About Visual Impairment

Financial information is so often communicated in the written form, with statements, summaries, letters and other writings your client is expected to read. As age may also be accompanied by **visual decline**, you want to be conscious that some older folks have trouble seeing the page you have in front of them. It is fine to ask your client if they would prefer that you read the document to them.

And if you have a choice about the lighting in your office, **full spectrum lighting** is better than fluorescent for anyone, particularly those with visual losses. You can get at least one full spectrum light for your own office and use it when you review any written items with an older client.

Sometimes getting something necessary done can get lost when there is a vision problem. Pride and denial may be reasons vision impairment is not addressed. It may also be because the mobility-challenged elder is not able to get out and get the problem treated or addressed. Below is a real case example.

## Illustration

I was involved in mediating a dispute between a senior and her adult daughter, who needed a durable power of attorney signed. The mother, who was largely housebound and very stubborn, had not agreed to sign the essential paper her daughter desperately needed to help manage finances. I went to the home to meet the mother. In the course of our discussion I asked the mother what things she wanted right now. She mentioned audible books. That made me question whether her vision was still good. She did not wear glasses. As it turned out, she had not gone to the eye doctor for a very long time and she had lost her glasses. Her daughter never knew this, and her mother did not say anything about it until I asked her if she had trouble seeing the paperwork. I offered to read the durable power of attorney document to her line by line. She said that would be good. As I went through it, she kept saying, "That's okay." I asked her if she understood what each paragraph meant. She did. We had arranged to have a notary public on standby just in case we succeeded in getting the document signed, as it was not going to be valid unless notarized. She agreed to sign it, and we got the notary in right away. The DPOA was signed and done. This is an example of a senior's vision loss getting in the way of a legal solution to a serious problem.

## What You Can Do About Resistance

A competent advisor may try everything possible to get a client to cooperate in devising a solid plan for aging and possible impairment. You may offer again and again to help get the DPOA in place so you have someone to call. You may offer your client a privacy waiver document to sign, hoping to cover all your bases so you're ready when that client ages and declines cognitively. And some clients will refuse.

The resistant client who chooses to refuse your advice and helpful suggestions may set himself up for disaster. **If you have done everything reasonable, that is the most you can do.** Even the regulators with every rule and mandate for you about older clients do not expect you to work miracles with everyone. Some people are just plain difficult, and you are not going to change them. If you have tried everything we offer in this book, and your client declines to cooperate with any of it, you have done your job. It should be well-documented from the time you first approach your client with a plan to the last effort you make.

## Signing Off by Your Client

Undoubtedly, any experienced financial advisor has had clients who do not want certain advice. They do not use common sense. They pay you but ignore your skill and efforts to protect their finances. When it comes to best practices, of course you document your efforts and all of these important conversations. And best practices should also include a way to have your client sign off on their refusal to accept your offer to keep them safe. Your legal department can devise a document that holds you harmless if the client will not go along with what your office or organization wants them to do to stay financially safe as they age. We recommend that this be made a part of an overall senior program in your office. That way, your paperwork or electronic records will show your efforts, reveal the reasonableness of those attempts and will clearly show that your client would not go along. In that kind of situation, should untoward financial effects occur, you will be able to show that it was your client's choice, despite your best efforts. From a lawyer's point of view, as long as you can show that you acted reasonably, you should be fine. If your reasonable efforts to get a client to cooperate are well-documented and follow a written protocol for an overall senior policy in your office, all the better.

## SUMMARY

Older investors are living longer than ever. You may have a few centenarians in your book of business before long. Perhaps you have some already. Expect a few issues with these older folks and how they communicate with you. Your awareness of ageist attitudes, and willingness to check in with yourself to be sure your own attitude is fair, is a good start. Adapting what you say and how you say it to the senior is necessary, as memory loss, as well as physical impairments, become problematic. Your willingness to offer your patience and understanding of your client will go a long way in retaining that client for life. And it is more likely than not that as clients live to very advanced ages, a third party will be needed to help you with that elder. Getting that third party set up in advance is a theme throughout this book and is particularly important as part of effective client communication.

For those very resistant clients, simply put, you may have to give up on trying to get them to do the smart thing. Planning ahead for possible incapacity is not for everyone. But you do need to make a good record of all your reasonable attempts to protect them. Finally, it is best to have a legally sufficient document, created by your legal department (or available as part of a policy initiation program from us), that your client signs, verifying that he wants no part of your reasonable efforts to have access to a third party when the need may arise. That will protect you from future untoward effects of his stubborn refusal to do the wise planning you want him to do.

**Quick Tips List**

In a nutshell, here are best practices for communication challenges with aging clients.

**1. Set a Date to Discuss Appointing an Agent**

Because many seniors resist talking about finances with family, get involved in encouraging the conversation. Plan a time and set a date to ensure that your client has appointed an agent on a durable power of attorney document.

## SUCCEED WITH SENIOR CLIENTS

**2. Use Trust to Persuade**
If you meet resistance, use persuasion: There is power in your trusting relationship. Talk about not wanting to burden her loved ones and ask what would happen in an emergency.

**3. Emphasize the Need for a Third-Party Involvement**
Always have a third-party contact on file to reach out to when you have concerns about your client's cognitive ability. Without it you will be stuck if your client can no longer make decisons.

**4. Consider That Some Clients Are Too Resistant to Cooperate**
Document all your efforts to plan for protecting them even if they refuse. You can prove that you tried.

**5. Accommodate for the Changes of Aging**
Make your office senior-friendly and adapt to clients' aging: accessibility, working with hearing and vision changes, and slowing your pace.

# 5

# YOUR CLIENT'S FAMILY: AN OPEN BOOK OR PANDORA'S BOX?

**INTRODUCTION**

Clients' families can be a source of cooperation and support for them or a constant source of stress. In this chapter, we discuss the various considerations about families of older investors and why they need to be involved when possible. Although many families do not function well together, there are ways to reach agreements even among those who have had years of conflict. Financial advisors have a role with clients' families as they age. Not only do we consider the wealth transfer issue but also the desire to keep a client's wealth from being decimated when transferred due to lack of communication. We walk you through the pros and cons of involving family in discussion of clients' finances and what you can do with problem families.

**Should You Involve Your Client's Family in His Financial Affairs?**
Because we are now experiencing the greatest transfer of wealth in our history, the financial industry has placed a lot of emphasis on the prospect of client retention with your client's heirs. Succession planning for businesses, "getting to know" your client's family and other axioms suggest you should not ig-

nore the family. Other than addressing your desire to keep your client's assets under management after he passes, there can be an additional motivator for engaging the family. That motivator is that you may well need family members to help you if your client becomes impaired.

Engaging the family while your client is fully competent serves two purposes: First, it establishes a relationship that can create trust and an understanding on the family's part that *you* are the right one for the financial management job. Second, it enables you to create an ally in the person whom your client has appointed as successor trustee or the agent on the DPOA. Usually, though not always, the appointee is an adult child, or other family member your client trusts, to do the job, if needed. An ongoing relationship and regular communication with your client's appointee helps you when a client shows those red flags mentioned in Chapter 1.

Because there may be mitigating factors in situations that look like cognitive impairment, a family member can fill in missing information and help you make a decision about how to address such problems as memory loss or confusion. Clearly your competent client will need to give you permission to include a family member, or more than one, in discussions about the assets you manage. Getting permission to speak to a third party is crucial as your client shows signs of diminished capacity. In an ideal situation, your client gets along well with her appointee on the DPOA or the trust, and the ongoing engagement of that person with the advisor sets up a helpful process for succession of management for the advisor. It also allows for educating the appointee as to what he may inherit, and how to preserve and grow it. However, as many of us have dysfunction in our own families, we know that our clients do, too. Family involvement can be helpful as much as it can be explosive and destructive. Beware of this, and make no assumptions.

## Connecting With Your Client's Family

If you studied finance, business or other related courses in school, you probably never got any instruction on the so-called "soft skills" involved in successful communication with families or in conducting family meetings. Your client is typically your main or only focus, and sometimes you don't even know what family the client has. Now that people are living longer than ever before, the need for these soft skills becomes increasingly important. The risk of cognitive impairment accompanies your client's longevity. Those who constantly research how to extend our life spans seem to forget that the risk of dementia rises with age. Longevity is not so great when the elder is seriously impaired, particularly in the area of cognition. Our society and our financial institutions have not provided well, when declining mental status demands it, for transitioning the patriarch or matriarch in the family out of the seat of power over financial decision-making.

Estate planning usually addresses the issue inadequately. In a typical estate plan that includes a trust, the trustee, who is normally the patriarch and/or matriarch, must either resign voluntarily as trustee or they must be found incompetent by a medical doctor, or two, when they can no longer serve as trustees because of incompetence. This typical kind of plan is likely based on the way things used to be when people did not live as long as they do now. When life spans were shorter, not as many people lived long enough to develop dementia, which can emerge with long life.

As we have pointed out previously, cognitive decline typically happens slowly, with symptoms worsening over a period that may span years. When the family elder lives to be 85, 95 or 100 years old, we often see an impaired aged person still in charge of the family finances, regardless of lack of judgment. Everyone involved in the elder's life is stuck with this situation, unless someone takes on the often onerous task of getting the elder to not one but two doctors, depending on how the trust is drafted, and asking the doctor to state in writing that the elder is no longer competent to make financial decisions.

When an elder does not realize there is anything wrong with his judgment, he refuses to go to the doctor for assessment of his cognitive ability. Sometimes the problem is compounded by the doctor, who doesn't understand how impaired the elder actually is in the few minutes she spends with the elder. Or the doctor may not want to be involved in the question for various reasons. Worse than anything, the doctor with a long-standing relationship with the patient may not want to say that his patient is impaired and will not pursue testing to get more data out of loyalty to the patient. The question of cognitive impairment may be simply swept under the rug or not addressed.

In our work we review numerous trusts for exactly the language that governs when an impaired elder should no longer be the trustee of the family trust. It is rare to find a trust that spells out in clear terms what should happen during that "grey zone," when an elder is partially competent but probably no longer has the judgment to make safe financial decisions. It may be the financial advisor in the elder's life who has spotted the red flags over time and, with appropriate permission, should bring those warning signs to the appointed family member's attention. We hope that advisors will be that attentive person who speaks with the family and develops a plan for transition of power over the funds she manages before the elder declines further. It can be done.

## What Family Business Succession Planning Misses With Aging Clients

Succession planning with a family-owned business typically focuses on transitioning the heirs to manage the business entity.

It rarely focuses on what the matriarch or patriarch want to arrange in the event of their own potential mental decline. This subject is simply too painful to face for most people. How many clients have you ever met who raised the question of their own potential incapacity for making financial decisions? Probably none. We can discuss our business management, the responsibility of our heirs, teaching the next generation and other related matters, but we avoid the truth: Any one of us can become cognitively impaired before, during or after the date of retirement. Family succession planning is great, as it permits a smooth transition out of any family-owned business with a well-thought-out method. But what if the patriarch or business owner suffers dementia before the plan is launched? This is our focus in this book, that we all need to plan for our potential loss of decision-making ability, and we need to outline how and when we want those around us to address it.

We urge financial professionals to be the leaders in bringing up the subject. It is a matter of including it, along with other discussions about how assets will be transferred between generations. If ordinary succession planning includes the assumption that the matriarch or patriarch will be fully competent through every part of the succession plan, that plan lacks an important contingency: What if they are not fully competent at some point? What then? This is where excellent planning needs to be done. Just as the best estate plans are creative and address the possibility of mental incapacity in a thoughtful way, so must the succession plan for any client's business include this.

What if the elder develops dementia? When do you have someone else assume the reins? What are the markers you use to make that determination? There is a phenomenon called "early onset dementia." For those cases, the symptoms emerge in a person's 50s, or even earlier. What devastation this can create if everyone has planned that she would retire at age 65, and no one has considered what would happen if she does not make it that far. And it is not just dementia. We have significant health risks in our country for heart attacks and strokes, both of which can disable a person and affect mental capacity one way or another. We need to be realistic. Longevity planning is a lot more than seeing how to make the business continue and to make the elder's money last.

## The Gap in Estate Planning

Even when a family sees an indication of cognitive decline, no one knows just when it is time for the successor trustee or appointed agent on the elder's DPOA to take over. Family may recognize the problem and be concerned about it, but they usually want their spouse or parent to remain independent as long as possible. So they do not act, waiting for "something to happen." Families are not better educated about the red flags of diminished capacity than financial advisors. No one provides a timeline, or criteria to use for the family or appointed person to understand the trigger point: when the successor trustee should step into the role of trustee, replacing the parent. There may not be a single trigger point. Usually the transition takes place after a series of mishaps or mistakes on the part of the elder, when family reach the point of being fearful that their parent is going to lose everything or get into financial trouble. Sometimes the trigger point comes only after the senior has been financially abused or manipulated.

Estate planning attorneys are very clear about who the client is and who it is not. The attorney's client is the elder for whom they have drafted the trust and other documents. The attorney preparing the estate plan has an ethical obligation to the client to meet with the client outside the presence of others.

The lawyer's duty to the client does not extend to anyone else, even if the lawyer is aware that the client has family who will have to be involved if the client loses financial capacity. The estate planning attorney may include the family in attorney-client meetings if the client wants this or insists on it, but it does not usually happen in the absence of a request from the client.

The estate planning attorney's responsibility to the client ends for estate planning purposes at the time the estate planning documents are completed and signed by the client. They will contact the client from time to time to update the documents and incorporate any changes, but those contacts are typically few and far between unless changes are more frequently initiated by the client. Attorneys rarely instruct the successor trustee, who is an adult child, about how to take on that job or when. They do not embrace instructing the successor trustee as part of the estate planner's job. The estate plan covers the necessary legal documents but does not do anything for the non-client, the heir of the client. That heir is often confused about stepping into unfamiliar territory, taking over decisions the parents have historically made about their money.

It would be exceptionally helpful if the norm were for lawyers to first get permission from clients to include the family in all essential estate planning discussions, invite the patriarch or matriarch to teach the heirs about the estate and prepare them for what the future might bring. It would also be very useful for the attorney to instruct the appointee about how to take over responsibility, what the duties of the successor trustee are and how to act in the best interests of the client at all times. That is not how it happens most of the time. The adult children, or other appointees, are left to guess, figure out incompetency on their own or hope that the aging parent stays healthy until the end of life. And millions of Americans do not remain competent for life.

As we described in Chapter 1, the dividing line between competency and incompetency is unclear. This leaves families wondering if they should step in now or wait until things get worse. The dilemma is compounded by an aging parent who does not think she is impaired. She resists all efforts to help with anything, even bill-paying. She insists on independence with her finances, even when it seems clear to everyone around her that she should not be handling the checkbook or investments any longer. The consequence is that assets are neglected, value is lost and the risk of financial abuse rises steadily.

Estate planning attorneys may be very well-meaning, and most do a fine job of drafting the estate documents for their clients. But they, too, ignore that "grey zone" of partial incapacity that happens to some people as they age and start to lose their judgment and ability to manage finances. They do not usually think through what would happen if a client with dementia refuses to go to a doctor and be declared incapacitated, thus allowing him to continue to manage his money when he is no longer competent. They do not often consider that some people cannot perceive their own mental decline. They do not address this with family at all. It is not usually found in a trust document, which only addresses incapacity in terms of what a doctor or doctors would say. That is indeed a gap in planning. Too many elders refuse to be evaluated by a doctor.

**Illustration**

Only once have we seen an exceptionally well-done estate plan that allowed for this possibility of a client refusing to go to a doctor. The client in question had signed special wording in the trust when fully competent. Years later he developed Alzheimer's disease, but he thought he was just fine. His wife was beside herself with fear of what he would do. He was still going to work but was not able to be effective in any way, and his employees were stealing from him. Fortunately, his very wise lawyer had put into the trust that if one spouse became incapacitated, in the opinion of the other spouse, the unimpaired one had to request that her spouse see a doctor for evaluation. If he refused, the trust stated, the full power of the trust would automatically pass to the other spouse within 30 days. Brilliant way to meet the refusal to be examined head-on, we thought. And it was. He did refuse. She became the sole trustee, after a written request to her husband that he be evaluated by a neurologist was refused. She was able to save him and, we hope, eventually save the family business as well.

**Expanding the Advisor's Role**
Advisors have a distinct advantage in these unclear situations where the client is somewhat competent but sometimes not, in that they see the client at intervals over time and can track red flags in a consistent way. They know how the client has functioned historically in making financial decisions, as the advisor has been involved in these discussions repeatedly with the client. Chances are the family has not had the same number, and extent, of financial discussions with the elder. **The advisor is in an excellent position to encourage the aging client to bring in the family at any point when memory loss, confusion or other problems appear to interfere with the client's best judgment.** An established relationship between the advisor and the family members makes this infinitely easier. The advisor who is well prepared has anticipated the possible decline of her client and has the contact information, as well as a prior acquaintance with the family, to lay the groundwork for a fruitful family meeting about their aging loved one. We have met forward-thinking advisors who make family meetings routine. The transitions are

smooth, because family has always attended meetings, and the elder feels safe in confiding in the advisor as well as the successors to his wealth. Family meetings are a key element to these smooth transitions of power.

## The Elements of a Successful Family Meeting

Transitions that involve family should also involve advance family meetings for the purpose of preparation. Some guidelines will help you have successful meetings, keeping your client's preferences and personality in mind.

### Timing

The family meeting should be arranged at a time that seems optimum for the aging person in the picture. Some aging people have preferences about the time of day they want to do business or be available to you. Honor their preferences as much as possible. When you can, ask other family members to **accommodate the elder's wishes**.

**You need an agenda**, even if it is only a couple of items. One might be looking at the future for your client's physical needs. Another might be the question of when it is the right time for the adult child to assume the role of agent on the account you manage, just in case the need arises. Everyone who is invited to participate in a family meeting about your client's finances needs to understand why you have called the meeting. If possible, your client should invite them. If he is unable or unwilling to do this task, offer to do it for him. Set a date and time, and **ensure that all family members he wants to have present have the same information about the meeting.**

A first family meeting should **be brief**. You cannot cover every possible issue about the family finances. Stick to a limited number of agenda items and introduce them after you welcome the participants. If your purpose is to communicate your observations about your client's diminishing abilities, you will need to have your client's approval to say this. It is never easy for anyone to admit that he is losing independence, but some elders must be guided to acknowledge and accept this reality. If your purpose is to educate your client's heirs about what the assets are and how you manage them, keep it simple at first and assess the level of interest on the part of the heirs. Financial competency is not for everyone, much as we wish it were.

Once you have determined who is interested in the financial matters introduced, you can **set another meeting, if your client approves**, to further educate those involved. This can continue for as long as the process takes to accomplish your purpose. Preparing your client's heirs, both for the parents' transition as well as to receive wealth, is not a short-term process. Depending on the number and complexity of the assets, preparation could take place over months or years. We point out that the advisor is in a unique position to know and understand the client, to encourage a high level of communication with family and to facilitate the process of building relationships with those family members most likely to take charge if the client's capacities diminish. While building relationships, the opportunity to create a process for education of your client's heirs presents itself. It can do much to reverse the current failure rate of intergenerational wealth transfers.

## What to Do With a Difficult Client

You may have a client who isn't interested in sharing personal information about her competency or details about her assets with the rest of the family. She balks at the very idea of a family meeting. If you are able to be persuasive, you may be able to get her to agree to meet with just one person in the family whom she trusts. That is a start. We again emphasize the high importance of having written permission from your client, while he is still competent, for you to speak to a third party. If your client refuses a family meeting, and the refusal is based on developing dementia and the inability to see the need, you at least still have the option to contact the third party your client appointed earlier. The written permission is your safeguard, and your client's as well. If you use your client's written permission, you can have a confidential conversation with the appointed person and share your concerns about competency, memory loss or whatever you have observed. Perhaps the client is being financially abused by someone. You could potentially stop it by your prompt communication with a family member, or appointed other, who can take action for your client.

Difficult clients who refuse to allow you to share any information, when you have valid reasons to be worried about their capacity, are not being rational. They do not perceive the danger to their finances that you see. Dementia or some other factors have compromised their reasoning abilities, and it may thwart your best efforts. You cannot likely dissuade them from irrational beliefs or resistance that becomes entrenched due to brain disease. However, once you have permission, you can contact that appointed party and work together on the best strategy to protect the aging client. You may not always succeed, but you do have a reasonable chance of taking action if you have done your homework and gotten that permission in place before any crisis.

**What to Do With a Difficult Family**

Given the divorce rate in this country, we know that there are a lot of second and third marriages, step-siblings and stepparents, and sometimes mistrust when divorce and remarriage involve long-standing conflict. The "get to know your client's family" adage is fine when you can do that without opening Pandora's box. But when your client has told you that she can't stand her second husband's children, or that she isn't speaking to her brother, who is supposed to be a co-trustee with her on an impaired aging parent's trust, the prospect of getting to know anyone in the mix is daunting. You may get along well with your client, but the family may be another story.

Your client's family may or may not be difficult. You need to find out how they get along as your client ages, because it may be inevitable that one or the other family member will be involved with your client's assets sooner or later. Either you will want to ask someone to step in because of your client's cognitive impairment, or an appointee may contact you one day and inform you that she has taken over, as successor trustee, all the assets you manage in the trust, and you will now be communicating with her and not your client.

**Can You Get Paid for Doing This Family Stuff?**
You may be wondering how you can get paid for spending the time it is going to take to get involved with your client's family. You may wonder, even if you had a way to be compensated, how you will find the time for the exercise, which could be complicated. There is no easy answer to either question. However, if you are planning to assist your high-net-worth client's family to prepare for the wealth they will likely receive, you could certainly set up a plan, for a fee, to do so. Depending on the asset classes involved, preparing heirs could take years.

One existing model is to charge a percentage of the net worth that is to be transferred. The process of preparing heirs in high-net-worth families has been studied, and successful approaches exist, though we do not address the "how-to's" fully in this book. **(At AgingInvestor.com we do offer an online course, "Best**

Practices For Success With Family Meetings," on this subject. Find out more about the course at www.AgingInvestor.com/courses.)[20] In our view, the financial advisor is the director of the project, which involves teaching of heirs and practicing the skills they need to assume ownership of the family's assets. It also involves bringing in other experts, managers and advisors the family is already using to maintain its wealth across businesses, real estate and investment portfolios, as well as other assets. In that model the advisor is the initiator of the discussion, the planner of the process and the guide to keep the family on track with all other parties who help with the future transition of ownership. And that advisor charges a fee for the management of this project. If you are planning to take on a client's family for purposes of introducing yourself, giving them information about what you do and clarifying what would happen if Mom or Dad became impaired, that is not a lengthy discussion. However, if preparing heirs is also a goal, see it as a project, make some estimates about how much time you will need to spend and find a fee structure. It may be based on percentage, an hourly rate or a flat fee. Your experience, your skill level, the complexity of your client's estate and the relationships in the family will guide you in estimating what it will take for you to do this. It seems apparent to us that this is important enough, and worthwhile enough, as a service that you should be compensated for offering it as value added to your ordinary management over a client's funds. Managing assets is one thing. Managing family meetings is another, requiring commitment, skill and time.

### When Should You Introduce the Subject of Talking to Family?

If your client is aging, and you have already identified some concerns about her cognitive status and capability, finding the time to

---

[20] http://www.aginginvestor.com/courses.

engage family is essential. Do it right away. Otherwise the elder may continue to decline, and both you and the family are unprepared for any alternative structure of power that keeps the elder safe. Financial ruin can result. A good time to suggest that you bring a family member of your client's choosing into a discussion about the future is when your client reaches any marker of aging that seems convenient to you. It could be at age 65, when the federal government and state law recognize the client officially as an elder. It could be when your client retires from employment. It could be at any important birthday, when an adult child graduates from school, marries or has a child. Pick your own marker, and set a date so you won't overlook this need until your client has aged further and the risk of incapacity looms.

We suggest that you make this an office-wide or firm-wide practice and that all clients of a certain age are approached about this concept. Doing it according to a standardized schedule offers you the advantage of first, getting the necessary permission signed, and second, having a natural opening to setting up a family meeting. We suggest using the 65th birthday as the marker, simply because it has traditionally been associated with retirement and change. If your office policy incorporates this, you can create a standardized letter that goes out in advance of the birthday to advise your client that your office routinely meets with a client and family member, or members of his choosing, to discuss the future with him at age 65. Some will resist and refuse. Others will accept your leadership. For the ones who cooperate, you are on your way to the best possible planning with families.

## What You Can Do With Difficult Families

No one expects you to be an expert in family dynamics. However, such experts do exist. They are called family mediators, elder mediators, conflict resolution specialists or family counselors. If you need to get business done with your client's family, but family dynamics and old resentments are getting in the way, consider using a specialist to assist you. **Mediation is an effective tactic when conflict exists to get to resolution and agreement.**

Resolving family conflicts via mediation is not therapy. Without a doubt, some dysfunctional families we see would likely benefit greatly from family therapy. However, the ones who could probably benefit most from therapy are perhaps the ones least likely to seek that kind of help. There remains an unfortunate stigma on any kind of mental health help and need for such assistance. But mediation is different. It is not going to lead anyone who hears about it to conclude that a person engaged in mediation "must be nuts" if they need this help. After all, many divorces, labor disputes and international conflicts are resolved through mediation. It is one alternative to unresolved family conflict that avoids escalation of family dysfunction to the point of lawsuits and courtrooms. If your client has a problematic family, consider suggesting mediation to reach some agreements. The stigma attached to therapy is not likely to be there with mediation. When you know there is a dispute, this is one good option offering hope for resolution.

**What Is Family Mediation?**
Simply put, family mediation is a voluntary, confidential process in which a neutral outsider to the family brings the parties involved into a discussion, with the goal of reaching agreements. The mediator serves as a facilitator and guide. Families in conflict are generally unable to see anything from another's point of view. The mediator helps them do that, giving each involved person an opportunity to speak. Assuming that the matriarch or patriarch is competent enough to participate, this includes

the elders. When each party has a chance to air his concerns, talk about what outcome of the fighting he wants to see, the mediator may offer suggestions and encourage each participant to speak up. The parties themselves decide what they want to do about reaching agreements. The mediator is not a judge who determines who is right or wrong. Rather, the mediator is a skilled and trained professional who understands conflict and how to help other people unwind it. If you do not have the training and experience, please do not try doing it yourself. It is far more than a friendly discussion. And because it often opens up old, deep-seated issues, it can easily get out of control with an untrained leader.

Mediation is private. Typically the parties sign an agreement that nothing said in mediation can be later used in any court proceeding. This encourages full discussion of what causes disagreements and mistrust. One of the most important benefits of mediation is that, despite the reality that the parties may not like one another, they are often able to reach agreements about specifics. Here is an example of a successful family mediation.

## Illustration: The Warring Sisters

Three sisters are the daughters of Jacob, a wealthy restaurateur and landowner. He has begun to decline mentally. As he falls into what appears to be dementia, the daughters fight over who should be in charge of his property and who should control his money. He has appointed one of them, a professional, to do that job, but the other sisters disagree. The other two sisters, with a long history of not trusting this older sibling, get into a standoff with her as to what is going on with Jacob's money. Lawsuits are threatened. The financial advisor remains silent through all this and prefers to take direction from his impaired client, even though he knows his client has dementia and may not be competent. Finally the sisters agree that an independent licensed fiduciary will handle the finances, keeping all sisters informed as to the accounting. But the fight goes on over what is happening at the restaurant and the other businesses. The fiduciary sees trouble ahead. She asks them if they are willing to mediate their disagreements. They accept the suggestion.

Dr. Davis and I mediate the dispute over several sessions. All three siblings live at a distance from one another, so we conduct the meetings via Skype.™ With guidance and an opportunity to voice their mistrust and anger, they are eventually able to reach several agreements. Accusations fly back and forth. Putting unspoken suspicions of wrongdoing into words gives the three of them a chance to say what they need to say. They see that some of their fears were unfounded. The older sibling remains in charge of certain business decisions, while the fiduciary handles the day-to-day finances. The sibling who lives closest to Jacob agrees to keep the other siblings informed weekly as to all transactions.

This is working well, and is a large improvement over constant bickering and threats that marred everything before. The eldest sister lets the advisor know that they have worked it out for now and that he doesn't have to worry about the lawsuit they were considering among themselves.

**The Advisor's Opportunity**
The advisor for Jacob was aware of his daughters' mistrust of one another, and he could have anticipated trouble ahead if he had been willing to look. Instead, he clung to the belief that as long as his client could recognize his voice, and say "yes" to anything, he must be competent. Clearly this was not the case. At the same time, the eldest daughter told us that Jacob thought he lived in Mexico and wanted to call home to see how

the restaurant was doing. He lived a block away from it. There were more red flags than anyone could count. To make it even clearer, he had a diagnosis of dementia from his doctor.

The advisor had an opportunity to suggest a family meeting, or family mediation, long before things between his daughters deteriorated as they did. The advisor should have known that Jacob was impaired. His memory was gone, and he often forgot where he lived. But, as with many financial professionals, Jacob's advisor did not have a clear idea of what his role with the family should be. So he did not act. It was not until the fiduciary had control over the account that he began to wake up to the reality that his client was no longer able to make financial decisions.

Advisors are in a unique position as their clients age. The advisor often knows the client over time and is, in fact, required by the rules to "know your client." The advisor sees the client's patterns and understands the client's tolerance for risk. The advisor could not have missed Jacob's memory loss, and, by his own inaction, the advisor was allowing his client to become vulnerable to any sort of financial abuse, including family abuse.

The older sibling who took charge could have herself been an abuser. The advisor allowing the impaired client to continue with managing his own finances, without any conversation with any of his daughters, set Jacob up for numerous risks. If the advisor had cultivated a relationship with the daughters earlier in Jacob's life, he might have had a better idea of what to do when Jacob started demonstrating cognitive decline. By the time Jacob thought he lived in a foreign country, it was too late to start that conversation. Things in the family had already deteriorated. Fortunately for them, a fiduciary found a way to get them to a place of making agreements before Jacob passed away. Mediation for them was a good choice, with a successful outcome. The sisters did not walk away best friends. However, they were able to reach a workable plan for communication and financial management for the remainder of Jacob's life.

**The Privacy Issue in Families**
Current rules prohibit you from discussing your client's financial affairs with others. However, if your client is present for the discussions and gives you permission to have them, there is not a privacy issue. Before involving your client's family with disclosing your client's assets, be sure you have your client's approval in writing, even if he has given it verbally. That is the safest approach, in case any dispute over what should or should not be shared arises at a later time. In Chapter 6 we describe the requirements for a writing that formalizes the permission. A formal document will protect you from problems that could arise later if your client forgets that she gave you approval to speak with family members. Dementia can do that: wipe out a client's recollection that she, indeed, said it was what she wanted. A formal, legally sufficient document signed by your client will protect you against that possible occurrence.

**The History of Conflicts**
Some wealthy parents have a lifetime pattern of expressing love by giving money to their children. This obviously colors the relationships between parents and children. Some aging parents have never learned other ways to communicate caring for their offspring apart from giving money to them. This is a breeding ground for discontent in families, as siblings rarely are all exactly even in how they turn out financially as they mature themselves. When some fare better in life than others, the resentment over being treated unequally financially can become very divisive.

    The advisor is not going to resolve deep-seated resentments

in families, nor will a professional mediator. This is not psychotherapy with a long-term goal of improving relationships. Rather, the advisor can become a facilitator in communication about managing the elder's finances, regardless of who doesn't like whom. Handling business together, and defining roles in families about managing assets when the patriarch or matriarch declines in health, is not the same exercise as taking on the demons that may have haunted the family dynamics for decades.

The point of having discussions about family wealth is not to try for utopia. Rather, it is to aim for a workable division of labor, if that is appropriate. It is to ferret out who is interested in the various kinds of assets that require management. It is to determine who is capable and willing to take on the responsibility formerly carried by the aging parent or other. And it may include who is going to best care for the aging parent when care is needed.

**The Long-Term Care Issue**

Just as our society seems largely unprepared for the possibility of cognitive impairment in aging loved ones, it is likewise unprepared for the issues of long-term care. Even when people can afford long-term care insurance, only a small percentage of Americans carry these policies. The cost of care for those who do not have long-term insurance is paid out of pocket by most. The wealthiest insure themselves by having liquid assets to use for care as needed.

Think about those you know personally who have lived to be over age 80. Were all of them 100% independent until the end of life? Probably not. Most people need some care as they reach the age of 80 and above. The longer a person lives, the more likely it is that some kind of help will be needed. For those with Alzheimer's disease, the need for full-time, 24/7 care is inevitable if the person survives long enough with a disease that can last 20 years. In a recent discussion with a discharge planner who provides post-hospital services to aging people, I was told that a 24-hour service for an aging person living independently in a seniors community is $350 per day. That is for non-medical help at home, which does not involve any care whatsoever from a licensed nurse. That cost is $127,750 per year for so-called "custodial care." It does not include any out-of-pocket medical treatment that Medicare does not cover. When you add in the cost of supervision of the home worker, plus transportation, medication and non-covered services many elders need, such as hearing aids or dental care, you are easily looking at over $200,000 per year. That figure does not include the "normal" cost of living at home.

Currently one wealthy client we know of is receiving care at home from an adult daughter. She is spending $20,000 a month for all her needs, and she is not paying her daughter for providing her care. The daughter is in conflict with the manager of her mother's trust, containing several million dollars, over this. The mother is in her mid-80s and will probably not run out of money to live as she does, even if she pays her daughter for the help she gets around the clock. However, other siblings are angry about the cash drain, believing that "their" inheritance is being spent unnecessarily. Indeed, a significant part of "their" inheritance is being spent, but it is certainly necessary for the care, comfort and quality of life of their mother.

What happens in some families we observe is that the cost of care comes as a shock. Since the vast majority of people prefer to remain in their own homes as they age, the cost of receiving care at home can steadily deplete reserves. Medicare does not cover long-term care. The large drain on the elder's finances to pay for full-time care is another factor leading to family fights.

Simply put, some adult children get angry or fearful that the inheritance they were expecting is being reduced by something they did not plan on or expect.

The rapid depletion of an elder's resources to pay for care is a recurring cause of conflict. Some heirs refuse to accept that there is a real need for anything so expensive and insist that the elder is not impaired. Some take on the role of caregiver themselves, either full-time or part-time, to their own financial detriment. They then may expect a larger share of inheritance as a result of what they gave up. Views as to what is appropriate use of the aging parent's resources differ. Fights break out among the family members, and communication about the future deteriorates. All of these factors can influence the conversation when an aging client declines, lives on and on, and needs to spend more and more of her resources to remain safely at home.

To be prepared for the discussion, and for your own advice for senior clients, **it is important for every advisor to understand the essentials of the cost of long-term care.** Sometimes appropriate planning can avert conflicts in families. Every year Genworth, which sells long-term care insurance, publishes a survey that tallies the cost of various kinds of long-term care by state. Advisors who have this information on hand, in family meetings or meeting individually with a client, can at least show them the figures, even if they are sure they will never need long-term care. If the family is prepared with the data, and the need for long-term care does arise, it may change expectations about inheritance. Advisors need to know the costs of such things as home care, assisted living and other choices for aging clients in order to educate them and prepare both clients and their families. Use published data to educate yourself with actual figures.

## Unworkable, Uncooperative Families

Having worked with hundreds of family issues, as consultants and mediators of disputes, over a ten-year period, we can say with some assurance that there will probably be some families who are not amenable either to discussion or mediation.

They seem to prefer being locked in conflict, accusations and bringing up old resentments. Regardless of the risk to the family wealth by refusal to work out any agreements or learn about how to best manage inheritances, some family members flatly refuse to speak to one another. No matter how honorable your intentions, they will not accept help. If they lose their wealth as a result of this, it is their choice. You can't change them.

The studies on failed transfers of wealth in families pinpoint the cause of these failures. It is the **breakdown of trust and communication within the family itself**, rather than any problem with the estate plan or tax issue or other outside forces. But how can one advisor tackle a family history of dysfunctional communication that keeps a family estranged? You can't. It is probably not surprising that a number of your older clients are too fixed in their ways to want to change the way the family works internally when it comes to financial differences. Sometimes too much history of family fighting makes it impossible for you to do anything beyond offering to open the discussion. When that suggestion is rejected, you may not have any other choices.

## SUMMARY: Your Takeaways

Working with your clients' families is necessary for your ultimate success, particularly if you hope to retain the family's assets under your management after the matriarch or patriarch passes. However, things may not go as you wish with some families. One must eventually accept that the most difficult families make their own choices about failed wealth transfers, risks of abuse or other sad events, and your best and most sincere efforts cannot change them.

The following list identifies what you can do now, summarizing the points raised in this chapter.

1. Every aging client who has appointed a successor or agent on a durable power of attorney needs to **educate the appointee** about what to do if the need arises for that person to take over decision-making. The advisor can lead that discussion.

2. Consider that any family with adult children who will inherit their parents' wealth should be prepared to receive it. You can lead the way by **offering to open the discussion with your client** and his heirs about the assets and how they are managed.

3. **Assess the kind of family your client has** by asking her about the relationships among adult children, step-siblings, etc. If she tells you no one gets along, you know you are dealing with a difficult family, and you can try the option of family meetings or not.

4. When your client's family is unable to communicate to reduce conflict and make agreements, and they do not know how to change the dynamic, **consider a professional conflict resolution specialist** as a resource. If your client is willing, a mediator can do much to help those who are willing to work on agreements to reach them.

5. When you encounter a client family that is seriously difficult, **wants no help and refuses your suggestions**, it is perfectly

reasonable to **walk away** from trying to help and simply allow them to make their own choices.

6. Every advisor needs to **be familiar with the actual costs of long-term care**. Whether your client thinks he will need it or not, you can mitigate family conflicts and help your client do good planning if this is built into the longevity discussions.

# 6

# PREEMPTIVE STRIKE: HIT THE AGING CLIENT PROBLEM BEFORE IT HITS YOU

**INTRODUCTION**

The regulators' joint white paper, *Protecting Senior Investors: Compliance, Supervisory and Other Practices Used By Financial Services Firms In Serving Senior Investors*, was referenced previously. In it, NASAA, FINRA and the SEC all urge that industry professionals change the way you do business with older clients. They stress the importance of taking steps to implement a program that addresses the many issues we have raised so far, including diminished capacity and elder abuse.

The regulators list numerous ways firms are considering to remodel their supervisory and compliance structures to meet the changing needs of senior clients.

In this chapter we review two of the areas of the regulators' discussion and describe our view on how to effectively implement their concepts by creating a senior-specific program for your organization or office.

The regulators want a lot from you. We limit this chapter to just two of their numerous recommendations outlined in their papers. We hope you will consider taking at least some of the basic steps forward they want you to take after you see these things laid out. And in Appendix 3, we offer you a Quick Start simple checklist to use to build a foundation for a program in your own office.

## Communication and Training

The two areas we have selected to focus on in this chapter are Communicating Effectively with Senior Investors and Training Firm Employees on Senior-Specific Issues.

We chose just two areas, because it appeared to us that these are a reasonable place to start with the long-term task of putting a senior-specific plan into place. Anyone can do these things. They do not require years of study or great expense. They do require commitment and time. If you strive to make things better for your older clients, and want what is safest and best for yourself in dealing with these folks, this is a road map for developing an overall plan in your office. Remove randomness and start strategizing.

## The Beginning: Segregating Senior Investors

One of the first things a firm can do about its senior investors is to segregate clients by birth date and create a separate database for them. Then you can devise a tailored and separate way of dealing with them, based solely on age. Does this sound like discrimination? It is. Seniors clearly need to be treated differently from the rest of your client population for reasons we have presented thus far: possible diminished capacity, vulnerability to manipulation, the risk of dementia with aging, a gullible and trusting attitude shared among the older-age cohort and other issues. It is clear from the writing and suggestions of regulators that they expect you to give your aging clients special attention. And you can't do that until you identify them. This means having someone go through every file, pick out the clients who are age 65 (or 60, if you prefer) and put them into a category that is going to become the basis of your office senior-specific policy creation.

Why do we choose 60 or 65 as the age that defines an "elder"?

The law put into effect in 1935 initially defined people as eligible for retirement benefits, in the form of Social Security, starting at age 65. In 1965 Medicare came into being, providing health insurance to those defined as eligible, presumably retirees. The eligibility age at that time was 65, and it remains so today, though the designation of "full retirement age" is now 66 for some, likely to be raised more. Much has changed in our society since then, as longevity has increased dramatically. However, following what the federal government established as "retirement age," it also defined the age one was considered an "elder." Legislatures and courts have defined an elder as a person in need of special protection, presumably because of vulnerability associated with aging. Laws against elder financial and other abuse typically define an elder as a person age 65 or older.

The term "elder" is already in existence legally. We stretch the time back to age 60, because some regulatory trends point in the direction of having special, senior-specific rules apply to persons age 60 and up, and some have these rules apply to clients age 65 and up. To be safest, you can put your new senior programs in place for all clients age 60 and up.

Here are some of the regulators' suggestions about communication with this client population.

## Implement Increased Frequency of Communication

One of the specifics the regulators outline is for you to increase your frequency of contact with senior clients. They want you to know about changes in health, financial needs and life events, such as widowhood or having to move to a care facility. You accomplish this by **setting up a schedule for portfolio review, or even just a telephone contact, particularly designed to touch on the things you need to ask about.** For example, let's say you are already reviewing your senior clients' accounts twice a year rather than the annual review you do for all your other clients. That is one thing the regulators have in mind. You would select out the clients in this age group, and schedule your reviews of their portfolios and inquire about their general status every six months. Perhaps that means just one more phone call a year to each of them than you are already scheduled to have.

Another thing you can do to comply with their suggestions and recommendations is to schedule a call, on a quarterly basis, to all your senior clients with already identified issues. This is a subset of the over-65 group with whom you have some concerns. They may have some recently identified health problems. They may have lost a spouse.

Perhaps they seemed forgetful the last time you spoke with them. At that time you can ask a set of questions from a list you have in hand, being friendly, and "just checking in on you, Mary." Your list might contain the following questions.

1. How's your health lately, Mary?
2. Is the income you're drawing out meeting your needs now?
3. Are you having any special additional expenses in your life since we last talked?
4. Are things going okay with your living situation right now? Do you need any extra help at home?
5. If your client has lost a spouse, you might ask if anyone else in her life is helping out with keeping track of bills and accounting.

As you can see, this need not be extensive, nor will it take a great deal of your time to do this checking in. What it can reveal may be extremely important. It may tell you that your client's health is declining or that she is not able to stay on top of bill-paying by herself. All of these details are part of the big picture of understanding how to keep your aging client safer. Essentially, you are looking for special vulnerabilities that may arise between your calls.

**The Emergency Contact Person**
A critical step in aging client safety is encouraging each advisor to have an **emergency contact** in the file, someone your client trusts. We urge you to do this with every older client and to insist upon it. And we do not think that one contact name of a trusted other is enough. Unfortunately, the client most often names an adult child. Family members, as we saw in Chapter 3, Financial Elder Abuse: How You Can Fight the Crime of the Century, are the most frequent financial abusers. Therefore, we urge you to get from your client several names of people he trusts to do what is best for him. The trusted other should not be limited to an emergency contact. Dementia, due to its insidious development, is not an emergency until it is too late for your client to understand anything that is going on.

In the years prior to the point at which a client appears clearly to have dementia or cognitive impairment, you may have a serious problem with diminished capacity that might not qualify as a true "emergency." A person can be in the process of losing capacity for financial decisions for years, and you would need to contact the trusted other at the earliest signs, not the last signs.

**In short, we think you should do even better than the regulators suggest: We urge you to collect several names of trusted others, then to get your client's written approval to contact those individuals when you see fit, and, under the described**

circumstances, to have a discussion with your client. Whom to trust needs to be part of that discussion.

Another important piece of the picture of improved communication with aging clients is for you to encourage them to discuss their financial affairs with their heirs. You can be the catalyst in this process. Such discussions allow you to recommend that the client appoint a trusted other to serve as agent on a durable power of attorney document. Knowing that your client has done that essential thing, you have the potential to work with the appointed person in the event that your client becomes incapacitated for any reason, including dementia.

Without a DPOA, it is generally a messy legal problem for those who must take responsibility for an impaired elder. They may have to undertake the expense of seeking a guardianship in court to even have legal permission to make a bank withdrawal or sell a stock for the elder. If you know who the appointed person is, suggest a conversation with your client and that agent. Lay the groundwork for communication, should the need arise to have the DPOA appointee step in on behalf of an impaired senior client. There are challenges in doing so. We described communication solutions in Chapter 4, Tough Talk: Communication Challenges With Aging Clients. We hope you will put them to good use in this conversation.

## Training Firm Employees on Senior-Specific Issues

The second area of focus in this chapter about what a senior program should contain is training of your staff and management. Regulators keep reminding you that you need to reach outside your own industry to learn about issues for seniors. These issues are not a normal part of an advisor's education. Even if you have had an aging parent with all sorts of problems, including dementia, this does not give you a broad view of what you need to know about your aging clients. The training should come from people with aging expertise: gerontologists, lawyers who work with elders, psychologists, physicians, social service providers, senior housing specialists and family conflict resolution specialists, among others. If you want to gain expertise applicable to your own aging clients and build a program on that foundation, you must obtain special senior-specific training.[21]

The regulators want you to take continuing education courses on senior issues. They want you to understand seniors' special age-associated risks. They tell you that you should understand elder abuse, red flags of diminished capacity and best practices. Does that sound like what you are reading about now in this book? It should. In creating this book we went straight to the source, the regulators, for suggestions, and we are doing our best to enlighten you here as to what they identified as the most valuable information you need to get. We want you to put regulators' urgings into practice. And you may need more than this book alone can teach you. Other experts offer different perspectives.

## Other Areas of Concern for Regulators

In their publications, white papers and initiatives, the regulators repeat the same recommendations about various other areas that concern senior clients. Some of these are beyond the scope of this book. They include use of senior designations, marketing to seniors, suitability considerations, ensuring the appropriateness of investments, and conducting enhanced supervision and surveillance of senior investors' accounts. We encourage any firm, office or organization willing to initiate a senior-specific program to **include all areas the regulators suggest**. You create your own innovative program with the leadership of a few people.

---

[21] AgingInvestor.com online senior-specific course: Regulatory Changes Advisors Must Face With Aging Clients, http://www.aginginvestor.com/courses/.

## SUCCEED WITH SENIOR CLIENTS

### Who Are the Leaders?

Leaders in any organization do more than think something sounds like a good idea. Thinking you might want to get around to it obviously won't get the job done. We suggest that you first identify who in your firm or office is interested in developing expertise in aging clients. Who is motivated? Is it someone with a lot of older clients? Showing interest and offering willingness to be involved is the sign of a leader in this effort. Once those individuals are identified, they need to set a schedule to begin the policy development work.

### What Steps Are Needed?

**1.** Define the Why

The process of creating a senior program is not going to be a quick exercise. Some thoughtful sessions will be needed to get this done. After you create a working group of interested persons assigned to the task, you need to **identify why you are doing this** and put it in writing. What do you hope to accomplish? A statement of purpose is your foundation. A mission needs energy, and yours might be that the number of aging clients is growing and you want to keep them safe and do what's in their best interests. That simple kind of statement is enough.

**2.** Define the What

Your policy needs to address the concerns you have in your own office, not someone else's office. You need to focus on all the areas the regulators suggest, but not all at once. Start where you are feeling the most uncomfortable. Is it in being able to clearly identify the red flags of diminished capacity? You have a list of the red flags (see Chapter 1) and you can use them with descriptions for anyone to use in documenting what they see in clients. Make sure each advisor understands what they are and how to spot them. Uniform ways to document will help you.

We suggest using an office-wide checklist with standard words describing the general ways diminished capacity manifests. These include the cognitive signs, emotional signs, behavioral signs and indications of financial abuse that have already occurred. See also Appendix 1, **Checklist: 10 Warning Signs of Diminished Capacity,** which can serve as a ready-made checklist, and Appendix 2, **Checklist: 7 Warning Signs of Financial Elder Abuse,** to speed up your process. If those are the initial pieces of your policy, you're on your way. Now for the next steps.

**3.** Define How to Address Client Privacy

The privacy issue is a matter of great concern. In Chapter 3, in which we discussed financial elder abuse, we described how the regulators want you to report abuse. That is after the fact. By the time you report it, the money is gone. In your own office-wide senior policy, you can set out ways to stop it *before* your client is abused or when you see the first suspicious signs of abuse.

When you consider the rules that preclude you from discussing your client's financial information with anyone else, you may think that you can't ever call a third party for fear of getting into trouble. We contend that this is not true. The view that you must remain silent with your concerns about your client's possible cognitive decline overlooks an important power you have: You can ask for your client's permission to discuss his finances with someone else.

Not every client will agree, of course. But for those who will, we urge you to consider developing a **special privacy document** for your client to sign that allows you to reach out to the appointed third parties. You would exercise this permission at the point at which you become concerned about your client's mental abilities.

The groundwork is laid by ensuring that everyone use the same words to observe and document both diminished capacity and suspected financial abuse. Further, you have some people in-house who have aging expertise through special training. When you create the privacy document, you include in it the things that would justify using it, to first escalate the problem, for additional opinions of those specially skilled in aging issues. Then, with consensus, you could contact a third party.

All of this needs to be built into the document you use for the necessary client permission to give up privacy. If this sounds complicated, it is. We experimented with it ourselves. Working with a team, we devised a model document for privacy waiver that we consider legally sufficient. It was drafted by lawyers. It is a part of our model template for creating a senior program in your own office.[22] Your legal department can assist you with building a necessary legally sufficient permission document. We consider it a central part of any senior program and one of the most important pieces of the policy you develop. With it, you can be proactive and reach out to third parties early, rather than after your client has declined as to be a danger to his very financial life. Without this kind of permission and program, you continue the status quo. Clients remain at risk. You remain at risk as well.

**Other Essential Steps**
Reporting:
In fleshing out your senior program, you will need to set out a plan for how to report elder abuse. When do you report your suspicions, and to whom? You can't stop it if you do nothing but observe it.

---

[22] http://www.aginginvestor.com/ten-step-policy-development-template-for-protecting-aging-investors/.

## SUCCEED WITH SENIOR CLIENTS

Communication:
You will need to establish an agreed-upon frequency of communication with all your clients of a certain age, which is 60 or 65 and above. Decide on some standardized scripts to use when making contact.

Account opening:
Plan for how you will **expand the information you get from every client** at account opening. Currently you are not required to obtain third-party information to open a file. You now understand how essential it is. Requirements do not say anything about a must-have for the third-party contact information, but you should include that. Figure out a way to go back to existing clients and get this additional information. If you do this across the board, you can let all clients know what is coming and why, so no one feels singled out. Account review is a great starting point. Subsequent follow-up calls also give you opportunities to get needed information in light of the risks of cognitive decline in the future. When this is a firm-wide policy, it will eventually improve your knowledge of every client.

### Escalation

Setting out the parameters of trigger points for escalation will also help you. And deciding who should review the matter once it is escalated, assuring that a senior-knowledgeable person or committee does this, will help you elevate the entire process to a level of excellence.

### Internal Aging Experts

Following the plan for escalation, we recommend creating your own panel of aging-trained advisors, compliance staff, risk managers or legal advisors to help you make decisions when you have identified a certain level, or number of red flags, or if you think there is financial abuse. That will help you make reasoned decisions about the next steps and to consult the person or committee who is the most informed regarding aging issues. These experts can offer everyone in the firm or office input and perspective about whether your concerns are valid, whether you can retain the client or whether it is indeed time to bring in a third party for decision-making.

You can develop your own internal aging experts, of sorts, with appropriate high-level training from **outside experts** in aging. This does not require a degree in gerontology or an advanced study of aging. Rather, it means getting a deeper knowledge of the very issues already discussed here: red flags, diminished capacity, the areas that make up financial decision-making and the possible other explanations for client behavior that concern you. Expertise in these specific focal areas is likely to meet your needs. The outside experts on aging train the trainers, who, in turn, train you. In the meantime, your internal aging experts are your resource to answer questions, offer additional perspectives and help you decide the best course with a particular aging client problem.

The ideal composition of your expert panel would be several interested, experienced individuals with different credentials. A compliance person, a client-facing advisor and a supervisor would be a great combination for your "senior- skilled" panel. The regulators have not spelled out who exactly should serve in this role. They do not want to restrict you. Rather, they want to encourage you to use your own human capital to develop the needed skill sets.

The regulators' suggestion that you have people around you with special skills is connected to the concept of a uniform way to escalate senior matters or impaired client matters. They do recommend that you have both an expert panel and a uniform way to escalate. Your expert panel would be the first step in the escalation process.

As it stands now, what we see as the most common way to deal with a cognitively impaired client is to wait until things have gotten really difficult with that client before it is escalated. We do not see uniformity in where the problem goes, step by step, after that. If it moves from the point of advisor alarm to compliance, there is nothing standardized about what happens next. We do not see aging experts in compliance departments. We see escalation as an examination of the question about whether retaining the impaired client poses a legal risk to the organization. If so, there are no identified interim steps we have observed. We do not see compliance departments involving a third party in the client's cognitive impairment problem as an option, probably because it is a nearly universal perception that privacy prohibits this. As explained above, we think this is a misperception, solved by advanced third-party contact permission from the client.

There may be some interim steps in escalation, including holding all transactions, but this cannot go on forever. Even if the client wants to do something financially dangerous, and the advisor and compliance are aware of it, suspending transactions does not solve the diminished capacity issues. There are vague descriptions, even in model rules proposed for the industry, about holding transactions for a couple of weeks or longer when a client is at risk. However, no one fills in the blanks in describing what is supposed to happen during the time that transactions are held up. From a practical point of view, **you have to know what to do during this time.** If you have the opportunity to get a third party involved, that is the most reasonable step. If abuse is at stake, reporting to Adult Protective Services may be the step you take.

Whatever the step will be, it should be part of a well-described and written procedure you follow.

Simply holding transactions does not, of itself, create any safety for the client. If an abuser is waiting for a good chance to manipulate the client, he'll gladly wait two weeks, or any defined period, to take another shot at getting your client's money. We urge being smarter than the criminals in this situation. If you intend to escalate a client's questionable condition or actions, have a goal in mind. If you want to retain the client, think of a substitute, appointed decision-maker who can come in and act on behalf of the client. Getting that individual involved should be a step in the escalation process. You can appreciate how important your client's permission is in all of this and why obtaining that permission in advance is paramount.

The ultimate step in the escalation process may seem to be to terminate the client. If you are working to avoid that, the involvement of someone other than your client in financial decisions is essential.

**The Successor Trustee on the Family Trust**

Sometimes a family member or appointed other comes in and assumes responsibility for your client. When a successor trustee becomes involved with the client's affairs, that does not typically happen at the request of the advisor or the advisor's compliance officer but at the request of the successor trustee. That individual may have entered the picture after a crisis, or abuse, or other triggering event. It may not be via a thought-out measured process, which we recommend as a better choice. The matriarch or patriarch of the family may not want to give up control over decision-making for investments. The successor may have had the client examined by a doctor, or two, and may have in hand a statement from the doctor that the client no longer has capacity for financial decisions. But this does not always happen in time to stop loss of funds through excessive spending, reckless charitable donations or predatory actions by ruthless family members and others. Sometimes the intervention of the successor trustee is well planned and organized over time. And, at other times, perhaps too often, the successor's involvement is reactive, because something harmful has already occurred.

## What Are Compliance Officers Doing?

In our review of studies on how compliance personnel think cognitive impairment should be addressed, it is clear that there is no consensus among various compliance officers. Therefore, we urge creating a policy that gives the advisor initial actions to take when the red flags are first noted. Specifying the number and degree of red flags should be a part of the escalation process. When a matter goes to compliance, there should be suggestions made that include alternatives to termination of the client. These must include contacting the third party your client appointed. Of course, the privacy issue must be clearly addressed before that, ideally at file opening. Failing that, the privacy issue and third-party identification should be fleshed out with every aging client at the time the account is reviewed.

The missing piece, as we see it, is the opportunity to address cognitive decline at its early stages, not when it is so bad there is no choice left but to get rid of the client. At an early stage in the development of cognitive impairment, the client still has some decision-making capacity remaining. The client may still be able to give you permission to talk to a third party. Your client may be willing to sign what we call a privacy waiver, allowing you to share financial information before he becomes the victim of financial abuse or before he loses control over his good decisions. **We want advisors to take advantage of the window of opportunity for protective and prudent action between the first red flag of diminished capacity and the point at which the client has lost the ability to make money decisions altogether.**

This window can last a few months or a few years. It could close rapidly if an otherwise gradually developing dementia is suddenly accelerated by a change in health status. These changes might take the form of a stroke, a head injury or fall, and even sometimes adverse after-effects of general anesthesia from an otherwise routine surgery. No one knows exactly what makes cognitive decline go faster. We do know that we have little or no control over its progression once it starts. Currently we have no medication that can slow the overall progression of dementia. What is important is that you can't predict how long you have to take action. You have no guarantee that next quarter or next year you will still have a client who is similar to how she is right now.

The benefit of a uniform escalation procedure applicable to aging, impaired clients is that the specially trained senior-knowledgeable panel to whom a matter is escalated is in a position to offer suggestions. Those suggestions would likely include contacting a third party. If the first person your client has appointed is a suspicious person, the hope is that an alternative contact is in your client's file. You would try that approach first. If it was not successful in enabling you to further protect your client, the matter would go back for further review by the panel with expertise. Perhaps they would recommend you suggest to your client a medical examination to check on her memory. If she complied with that, and agreed to share the results of evaluation, that would give you and your panel guidance as to what should happen next.

If the client declined all suggestions and refused to cooperate, the panel with expertise on aging issues might decide ultimately that it was time to terminate the client. But not every client who has signs of cognitive decline will refuse every suggestion you make. The value of your long-term relationship with your client is trust. Trust is leverage for you to make requests and suggestions to your client. Even in the early stages of cognitive impairment emotion remains intact, trust is felt and a client may be willing to follow your suggestions. When no standard way of escalating matters involving diminished capacity exists, there is no clear path to follow. The last resort becomes the first resort: If the client is a serious problem, get rid of her.

To Dr. Davis and to me, as outsiders to the financial services field, we see this as a huge area of lost opportunity. If advisors take the time and make the effort to recognize the early warning signs of cognitive decline, there is a chance to do three of the most important things the regulators want you to do.

- Take protective action when you can
- Involve a third party (one or more)
- Work with the third party to prevent financial abuse

Haphazardly noting that some aging clients may have dementia, and waiting for some kind of crisis before you act, is foolhardy and dangerous to the client's financial safety. Worse yet, without a policy about third parties, including privacy waivers, red flag identification and the like, you will end up with a client who may be too impaired to give you permission to do anything at all.

Bear in mind that the regulators' strong and repeated suggestions and recommendations about senior policy development did not come out of the blue. They seem to us to have arisen from the astonishing number of elders who are being financially abused from every direction. No one should ignore this, and they want you to take steps to show that you are not ignoring it.

**SUMMARY**

FINRA, the SEC and NASAA have all articulated a joint mission to ensure that senior investors are made safer by industry professionals. Their writings repeat the urging that all financial advisors take certain steps to create greater safety for their clients. Those steps are to be incorporated in programs firms adopt that include specific points. Among them are the following.

- Increasing the frequency of communication with aging investors
- Ensuring that every client has a third-party contact, identified in the file, for you to reach in the event of suspect abuse and when red flags of diminished capacity appear
- Getting training in senior-specific issues and creating a group in organizations that has extensive, high-level training in the area
- Additional areas of concern: marketing to seniors, ensuring suitable and appropriate investments for seniors, use of senior-related designations and enhanced senior investor portfolio reviews and surveillance. Creating a senior program for your office will take time, but the greatest motivator should be that you will certainly lose aging clients, and the assets you manage for them, if you do not have a senior program in place. Diminished capacity is too common, and terminating aging clients who have it is too inadequate a solution for you to continue with the status quo. We want you to get the ball rolling with a policy change, starting now. If you are pressed for time, see Appendix 3 for a Quick Start checklist anyone can use.

# 7

# THE ELEPHANT IN THE ROOM: ADVISORS THEMSELVES WITH DIMINISHED CAPACITY

**INTRODUCTION**
Age-related cognitive impairment is an issue that affects everyone. Parents and grandparents, elderly other relatives in our lives with dementia and other cognitive issues, are a reflection of what is happening across the entire population. Every profession will have some aging members who are suffering cognitive impairment. We have support systems to help with our family members, often connected to health care providers and social service agencies. We have caregivers to assist with those who can no longer manage independently at home. We have lawyers who specialize in elder law and provide needed legal planning and documents. But **we do not fully address the issue of how we as professionals should, or could, respond to signs of cognitive impairment in our own professional colleagues**. There is no agency in place that offers a clear way to treat a colleague financial advisor who is losing the capacity to make sound, reasoned financial decisions and recommendations for clients. This chapter is an effort to identify the problem in the financial services field, point out how pervasive it is and then to offer possible courses of action.

While writing this book, we were asked by an astute financial professional to speak about this subject of impaired financial professionals. He told us that there are people he encounters in the field who work as financial advisors long past their prime and who put their clients' financial safety at risk because of their loss of ability to do the job. Others we have spoken to about the subject of impaired colleagues have also agreed that it is a problem. No one informed us of any policy from institutions, legal departments, compliance or risk management about rules to protect a client when a senior financial advisor is showing signs of losing capacity. Only the most extreme matters are likely to come to the attention of legal or compliance departments in financial firms and institutions. That leaves a large untouched problem of advisors who may be gradually losing the ability to safely handle client finances.

We suggest workable solutions to take the problem in hand rather than ignoring it. Perhaps it is an ethical concern. Should we step in when we know a fellow advisor is no longer able to keep track of clients' finances? Is it our business? Perhaps it is a legal concern. Does the firm or office create legal exposure when an impaired advisor who is handling clients' funds demonstrates multiple red flags of diminished capacity? This is what we examine here. We hope that you will take some suggestions from this chapter and put them to work wherever you are. Client financial safety is at stake if we ignore the reality that some advisors should retire even when they do not want to do so.

**The Problem**

With our aging population, many professions are just beginning to address the issue of diminished capacity among their own. Pilots have long been subject to mandatory retirement at age 65. Surgeons over age 80 are closely scrutinized. There is no such mandatory retirement or age-related closer scrutiny for most other licensed professionals. As long as one complies with mandatory continuing education requirements, you've got that license for as long as you want.

And so far, we find no clear rules financial professionals face that require stepping down from a professional practice because of loss of mental capacity. Even advanced age itself presents risks, whether a person is cognitively intact or not. A 90-year-old will likely not process information at the same rate as a 45-year-old. And consider that advisors have no mandatory retirement age, no matter how slowly they work on client portfolios, no matter how poorly they understand what they are doing.

Statistics tell us that by age 85 one in three of us will develop Alzheimer's disease. For the years preceding a diagnosis of this dementia, the person who has this brain disease is gradually losing capacity for financial decisions. The decline can take place for many years before it becomes so apparent that everyone around the affected person is aware of the impairment. Financial professionals are not different when it comes to these risks.

Advanced degrees and sophisticated knowledge may give us more grey matter in reserve when the brain develops dementia, but these characteristics do not create immunity to dementia. An educated person may be able to cover up the symptoms longer, or adapt for a time longer with some impairment than one who is not well-educated, but certainly anyone who develops diminished capacity for any reason should not be serving in a professional capacity. The gradual development of disease in a formerly high-functioning and successful financial professional is particularly problematic. No one expects it. Few have any idea about how to effectively address the warning signs of impairment they see in their colleagues.

## The Question: What to Do?

As people are living longer than ever before, and the risk of dementia rises with age, some of our own fellow financial professionals are now impaired or are in various stages of developing cognitive impairment. It is inevitable. **What are we going to *do* about the impaired colleagues among us?** Some of them are still maintaining offices, serving clients and handling millions of dollars in client assets while showing signs of cognitive decline. This is not safe, of course, but it seems to be a somewhat untouchable subject. No one wants to talk about it. No one seems clear about how to bring it up. Clients whose funds are being managed over a period of years by their advisor may not be aware of an advisor's cognitive impairment. They trust the advisor. Client contact is infrequent. However, those who work more closely and frequently with an advisor in decline may be aware of the warnings and the changes.

Lawyers, architects, psychologists and other licensed professionals all lack any clear direction when one of their own demonstrates signs of declining capacity. There are few, if any, rules or regulations from licensing bodies that adequately address this problem. It is quite different from substance abuse or a mental health problem such as depression. Those can be successfully treated under the right circumstances. Dementia accompanying Alzheimer's disease cannot be successfully treated or cured at this time, as far as we know. Should you ignore what you see in your colleagues, or should you or the organization you work for take steps when warning signs of diminished capacity appear? Is it your business?

**We suggest that an impaired colleague is everyone's business.** A firm has other advisors who can step in and offer assistance in managing accounts when a colleague shows such things as short-term memory loss. There should be protocols in place guiding firm employees about what to do. We suggest some protocols later in this chapter. An independent advisor is more of a risk if he or she works alone. There are few, if any, professionals nearby to observe the advisor on a daily basis. But as dementia or other cognitive issues emerge, other professionals will see the solo advisor in the context of doing business with them, at professional meetings or social occasions. As cognitive impairment progresses, it is more likely to be observed by others who work with the affected person in any setting. Again, we believe informal protocols should be in place in the event that you, the financial professional, in any location see and become concerned about an impaired colleague. You, and the person you are concerned about, are better off if you have an idea about how to approach the problem, what to say and what other steps you might take. Your colleague's clients will be safer if you do take measures to protect the professional as best you can.

**Illustration: The Impaired CEO**

An example of what can go wrong when a professional is impaired, and no one knows what to do, is illustrated in this real-life example. We have changed the names but not the facts. The professional was a licensed architect and business owner. He could have been in any other kind of business, too. The issue faced by those around him is somewhat universal. A powerful and highly successful man developed cognitive impairment, and he continued to work, creating danger for many. Yet everyone hesitated to act until things had reached a breaking point. He was the company founder, the boss. No one wanted to question him. No one wanted to force him to retire. He thought he was fine. He had been going to the office every workday for 50 years.

We were contacted to assist with this complex matter. The architect had enjoyed decades of success in his field, designing hundreds of large projects. He began to show alarming symptoms of memory loss in his mid-70s. By his late 70s he was clearly unable to function as an architect. License renewal in his state was by computerized exam. He could not pass the test. His partners coached him, gave him sample questions and showed him how to answer them. Still he could not pass. This created a sort of nightmare in the company, as no one knew what to do with him, and no one had the nerve to ask him to step down.

His behavior had become irrational. He was harassing employees. He was losing his ability to communicate. He kept going to the office, because no one knew what to say or do to stop him. We intervened into a multi-layered situation involving partner conflicts, financial manipulation of the CEO, family disputes and many other related problems. Eventually, with extensive planning and intervention, he did leave his position. It took numerous meetings, a defined strategy to stop him from returning to work, and a team of professionals and friends acting together. Fortunately, he responded well to the actions of those around him, directed by a step-by-step plan we had introduced. Prior to that there were no rules in place, no provision for what to do in the event of his incapacity other than a corporate document that assumed he would voluntarily resign if he became impaired. He would not resign. This left everyone vulnerable to the effect of his diminished capacity. The consequences were expensive for everyone. This gentleman brought his company perilously close to legal liability for his strange and inappropriate behavior, driven by Alzheimer's disease.

This illustrates what lack of a plan can do, and how dangerous it can get, if no one speaks up or takes action. It is certain that the architect's colleagues knew that he was impaired years before his behavior got totally out of control. Neither his business partners, nor his corporate attorney, nor anyone else suggested that he retire at the time his impairment became very obvious.

The takeaway from this example is that, if an impaired colleague cannot pass a license renewal or complete required continuing education courses, he should no longer be allowed to function in his former role. Partners, colleagues, family and friends must take steps to stop the professional from continuing on as if everything is fine.

### Illustration: The Trial Lawyer With Dementia

A colleague attorney described working in his father's firm as his father grew older and began to fail cognitively. As his father, a prominent trial lawyer, began to show signs of diminished capacity, no one stopped him from continuing to represent clients. He had cases to try, with exceptionally complex issues to address. Sharp mental ability was crucial. His son, at the time a fairly new lawyer, had to take over much of his father's work, which became a burden for him. He was not experienced or skilled enough to do all his father had done. It was a daily struggle for the son. And he spent a lot of time covering up for his father's disabling memory loss and lack of mental sharpness. His father did not recognize that anything was wrong with him. He was a man of high reputation for success. No one in the firm, and no colleague lawyer, wanted to confront the reality that he had clearly lost his edge. Continued client representation was risky for the father, but it went on and on. The entire matter of his gradual decline was largely ignored, covered up and allowed until finally his son did assume full authority over his cases. Only under pressure was his father willing to stop practicing law. Physical failings, not his mental decline, ultimately forced the issue.

**The takeaway** from this example is that the trial lawyer could have been another kind of professional, giving financial advice.

He could have been working with a junior advisor who was just learning the ropes. Failure to address the obvious problem of impairment of a senior financial advisor could easily lead to very high-risk situations in which a client's funds are put in danger. The skills in giving financial advice obviously require full cognitive ability. A new advisor would not have the necessary skill and experience, or knowledge, of every client that a practiced advisor has.

Changing market conditions and products should be discussed with any client whose portfolio can be adversely affected by the economy at any time. But the ability to discern what advice to give, and when, requires sharp judgment. An advisor with declining capacity cannot exercise the necessary financial judgment to maintain essential professional responsibility for the client. As with a lawyer, diminished capacity in the practice of law can readily spell damage to a client's rights. With an advisor, diminished capacity in providing financial management and advice can likewise spell damage or destruction of a client's savings.

While a junior professional can certainly be of help, it is unfair and risky to place full responsibility for someone else's work on the shoulders of a young professional who is unprepared to manage it. It would be far better to have a **succession plan** in place that includes a provision for how a transition to another professional would occur in the event of unplanned incapacity. That is far different from planning retirement from one's business in an orderly fashion. An unexpected crisis can occur, as can a gradual decline in cognitive ability.

Plans should be locked in for either scenario.

### Illustration: The Financial Advisor With Dementia

Mark is a 75-year-old former bank president who enjoyed a very successful career with a large bank. He had no children and was divorced later in life. After retiring from the bank, he became a financial advisor and was quite happy in that career. He accumulated millions of dollars in his own investments and retirement accounts. But by the time he reached age 70, he began to experience problems with his memory. Nonetheless, he maintained his book of business, and continued making recommendations and decisions for his clients. Soon after he started to suffer memory-loss issues, he became involved with local charities and became a regular donor. Once he started this, his charitable giving steadily increased. Numerous large philanthropic organizations invited him to become a donor, and he never turned them down. He enjoyed the charities' enthusiastic welcome and response. He didn't keep track of what he was giving, but he thought everything was fine. After all, he was a wealthy man.

But he faltered at work. He kept forgetting things. He had trouble concentrating. Not aware of his decline, he kept working, managing money for numerous clients, oblivious to his problems. He lived alone. He had a brother in a distant city, and they talked regularly. One day his brother came to visit. He was shocked to see how Mark was living. Mark's nice apartment was a frightening mess, a disaster, and Mark had become a hoarder. His brother realized that the little things he had been noticing over the last two years were indications of a larger problem with his brother. Mark wasn't just forgetful. There was something really wrong here. He obtained power of attorney and looked into Mark's finances. He discovered that Mark had given away millions of dollars. With considerable effort, his brother convinced Mark to retire from his business. His brother had Mark evaluated by a doctor, who diagnosed Mark with Alzheimer's disease.

Mark's memory continued to decline steadily. He and his brother had a falling-out. He then moved again to another state to live with his sister. By this time Mark was 78 years of age and needed to have supervision on a daily basis, as he would forget to eat or bathe, unless reminded. His sister got power of attorney and took stock of his finances. Mark had less than a million dollars left at this time.

Other than his dementia, Mark was in good physical health. He might live a long time. His sister put him into an assisted living facility with a "memory care" unit. She realized that as his care needs increased, and if he lived long enough, he could run out of money altogether. She described, with some sadness, that if he did run out of money, she and her husband could end up supporting this once-wealthy man.

**The takeaway** is that the signs of Mark's memory problems became obvious after a time, and these would have been visible to his colleagues. He was a very social person and interacted with other advisors quite often. His clients' portfolios were endangered by his Alzheimer's disease. How can a person with serious memory loss be responsible for managing client funds?

It may have been possible to stop Mark from giving away most of his wealth, leaving him vulnerable, had someone acted sooner to find out what was going on with him. In his case, family was able to persuade him to give up his business and retire completely. Sometimes it will take a combination of family, doctors and professional colleagues to persuade a person with dementia to stop working. If a trusted other has power of attorney, that person is in a position to stop the overly generous, unaffordable giving in which Mark engaged to his own detriment.

## Financial Advisors Starting to "Lose It": Do You Know the Signs?

Think of the consequences of memory loss, confusion, loss of ability to track the conversation and loss of financial judgment for an advisor managing clients' assets. In Chapter 1, we discussed what dementia looks like and the components of financial capacity in **clients**.

Consider how these very same issues will affect the work of someone who is in the advisor role. The most difficult part of determining whether a fellow professional is impaired or not is the subtle nature of the onset of dementia. How will you know? It doesn't just jump out at you, but there are signs. Being aware of them is a first step in managing this issue. By way of review from Chapter 1, you recall that the signs of cognitive impairment include the following.

**1**. Cognitive signs, such as memory loss and confusion, inability to track the conversation
**2**. Behavioral signs, such as unkempt appearance, changes in eating habits and hygiene
**3**. Emotional signs, such as uncharacteristic mood changes, outbursts, anger, irritability or being unusually withdrawn from others
**4**. Signs of financial abuse, which can include being taken advantage of by anyone, such as an unscrupulous family member, a care provider or a charitable organization exploiting a person who does not keep track of donations

You may never see all of these things at once in an impaired colleague. However, if you are aware of the changes that aging can bring, and you have a basic understanding of what developing dementia looks like, you are more likely to be able to spot the red flags in your own colleague.

No one is protected against dementia because of what we do for a living. No one is protected because we have college degrees or higher degrees. Some proportion of our population will develop dementia across all occupations and professions. Some financial advisors will develop Alzheimer's disease, and that brings us to the question of what to do about it. Here is food for thought. There are not exact, cut-and-dried answers for everyone. But there are options.

**Imagine This Scenario**
One of your older colleagues, Ralph, is developing some kind of cognitive problem. You're no expert on this, but things keep happening. You know Ralph through your work, and common interests, as financial professionals. You are friendly and always enjoy each other's company.

Perhaps Ralph forgets that you have a luncheon planned, which he agreed to attend, and then he does not show up. That can happen to anyone, so you don't think much about it. But it happens again. You agree to meet with him for another occasion. He confirms it. And he is not there at the time you agreed upon. When you ask about it, he has a blank look on his face. He totally forgot and does not remember confirming the appointment. That makes you wonder.

Later that week Ralph is telling you a story about a client. It had a funny element in it, and you got a chuckle out of it. You run into Ralph the next day and he tells you the same story again, not remembering that he saw you the day before and that he told you the story then, too. You remind him that he already told you about that funny client. He quickly changes the subject, or apologizes and says he didn't sleep well the night before, or some such explanation.

A couple of months later, you and Ralph go to a conference on the latest tax considerations in financial planning. You're seated next to him. He nods off during the presentation, which is in the 9 a.m. session. Later you are discussing one of the suggestions the presenter made, about your own tax-avoidance planning with your clients, and you ask Ralph if he thinks he'll incorporate that suggestion. He gives you a non-answer and immediately switches to another subject. You get the impression that Ralph didn't get anything out of what was, to you, a very useful presentation. You are now beginning to think that Ralph has a real memory and concentration issue going on. You keep seeing little signs, but now it's more obvious than ever.

You've known Ralph for over five years. He is not a drinker. You know he has what seems like a pretty good life, and he doesn't seem sad or depressed. He's physically in good shape. He's 73 and plans to work for at least five more years, as he loves being a financial advisor. But the forgetting is happening regularly as time passes. Now you are aware of it over and over, and reminding him is not helping. He goes to a firm social event and can't keep track of the small talk. He was always a social guy. Now he just stands around, not talking much. Something is wrong, you think. But what?

Sitting down with Ralph a couple of weeks later, you tactfully mention to him that he seems to be missing a lot of appointments you have had with him lately. "Is something going on?" you ask. Ralph assures you that he's fine, and everything is fine, and makes a joke about missing a few appointments. He's a very busy guy, he reminds you. You talk about something else, and he seems to lose what you are saying, asking you to repeat it. He just seems to be "spacy."

You know that Ralph has a very large book of business. He's been an advisor for 35 years. Do you have a responsibility to do anything about what you see? He has a lot of high-net-worth clients. He is giving them advice every day. Is that safe? If he can't keep track of what you say, and often can't remember things that happened recently, how is he dealing with the clients' portfolios? You ask yourself: "If I were Ralph's client, would I notice there is something wrong?" or would the clients just accept his advice as they had for years without question? **How long would it take before Ralph's memory and judgment were so damaged that he did something that caused financial harm to a client? Are you supposed to do anything, or say anything more to Ralph, about this? Should you tell anyone? What do YOU think?**

**Advisor Responses**

In polling financial professionals in larger, medium and solo offices, we got the following responses to this question of "What would you do about an apparently impaired colleague?" We offered them the scenario of Ralph, above, and asked for their comments. The prevailing response, we were happy to hear, was not to ignore the problem, but to act.

**Large institutional wealth manager:**
*"I would feel obligated to bring it up to the management team immediately to assess his competency. This would likely not only likely reduce the probability of a client suffering substantial losses (and perhaps ultimately the firm) but also Ralph and his family's financial future."*

**Independent advisor in a solo office:**
*"I would have done something the first time I noticed real cognition issues. I would call an expert for advice, or, if that weren't available, I would have taken it up with Ralph. If there was not acknowledgment and a proper course of action with Ralph, I would have tactfully taken it up with the appropriate firm resource before something unfortunate happened with a client. This would be the right thing to do for Ralph (orderly transition of clients), clients and the firm."*

**CFP in a medium-size firm:**
*"I would absolutely be compelled to say something to someone besides the individual, starting with our chief compliance officer. As a professional, I'm required to act in the utmost good faith, in a manner I reasonably believe to be in the best interest of the client. I couldn't, with a clean conscience, not say something."*

## Ethical Considerations

The financial professional has no clear guidance in the ever-widening web of rules and regulations for your industry to tell you what to do when you see or suspect diminished capacity in a professional colleague. As we see more aging professionals, we need to develop protocols to address how to keep them from making preventable mistakes and from hurting themselves, the clients and the office or firm where they work. Where can you go for guidance? If your compliance department does not have clear protocols about this issue, they may struggle, too. If the idea is to have Ralph assessed, what tools will the committee use to determine Ralph's capacity? And what if you say something to Ralph, or to anyone in a position to address it with him, and Ralph says he is just fine and please don't meddle in his business? This can be tricky for anyone to confront. Discipline may be required or be a last resort.

Resistance from the impaired person is something you should anticipate and have a way to work with, as it is an expected response to being told one is apparently impaired. And, as pointed out in Chapter 1, Ralph's symptoms could be due to numerous other factors that do not mean he is impaired. These include medication side effects, illness and other possible causes. These other possible explanations for his behavior should be ruled out before one assumes that he has cognitive decline. Going through the other possibilities with Ralph that could explain what is going on should be the task of the reviewer, committee or compliance personnel when they look into what should be done.

## What Do Lawyers Do With This Issue?

Some effort to address age-related impairment exists in the legal profession. State Bars and the American Bar Association have their own Lawyer Assistance Programs, or those designed for both lawyers and judges. These exist primarily to assist lawyers who have substance abuse, addiction or mental health issues. But age-related issues are now a part of what these programs also hope to address. Counseling and confidential group support is available in these organizations. Can we learn from the legal profession, and can what they do also apply to financial professionals? We think it can. At least someone has forged a path and made efforts to create ways to help impaired colleagues. However, in researching the question of diminished capacity, we found no sample script or clear protocol describing how a lawyer might address another lawyer who seems to have dementia, diminished capacity or any form of cognitive impairment that would interfere with effective client representation. That may be the initial obstacle: Who is going to speak up if a fellow professional seems to be impaired? And how does the professional who may want to speak up manage the discomfort that comes with bringing up such a personal subject with a colleague, particularly one who is a friend?

## Things We Can Borrow From the Legal Profession

The largest voluntary organization of lawyers in the U.S. is the American Bar Association. It has a commission that did address this issue of the lawyer impaired by age-related conditions. Presumably, the age-impaired lawyer has done something wrong that is visible to others around her. When any sort of serious misconduct occurs, fellow attorneys are required to report the misconduct to another attorney, regardless of age or seniority.[23]

Under the same model rules, a supervising lawyer or partner is required to take remedial action when the lawyer observes the non-serious misconduct of another lawyer. However, the rules do not squarely address what must happen when the person with the non-serious misconduct is the senior attorney, supervisor or partner himself. This is exactly the issue we address here. Both the legal and financial services professions (if not all professions) must develop specific ways to protect the clients of the firm, or the individual professional, when the age-impaired person is in a position to create harm.

One thing seems clear: We can't wait until hundreds, or thousands, of clients are adversely affected by impaired financial professionals to figure out how to address this looming problem of colleagues who may develop dementia. We suggest creating some office policies that take the risk of cognitive impairment of financial advisors into consideration. You may never need protocols, but if you do, you will be glad they are in place. We would not want to see you, the financial professional, in the position of the architect's partners in the illustrations above, should the architect be instead a senior financial advisor or broker-dealer in your own firm. Likewise, we would not want to see you in the position of the young lawyer whose father was losing capacity, overwhelmed when the senior lawyer was "losing it" and could not see that he was impaired. The junior person working with an age-impaired senior advisor should have a way to report the problem and protect the advisor's clients. And we would not

---

[23] ABA Formal Opinion 03-429("Obligations With Respect to Mentally Impaired Lawyer in the Firm") and ABA Formal Opinion 03-431 ("Lawyer's Duty to Report Rule Violations by Another Lawyer Who May Suffer from Disability or Impairment").

want Mark, as described above, to be the partner, or a fellow employee in your firm who starts to slide downhill, to continue to work, while no one other than family does a thing about the red flags they see. Family might not be enough. They did not see Mark at work. You could be an observer of a Mark in your own office.

**Possible Solutions: How to Report an Impaired Colleague and How to Protect Clients**
As we have no particular rules to guide financial professionals, we need to create some. If we start with how we assess clients for diminished capacity, as discussed in Chapter 1, we can apply the very same criteria to our own colleagues. Imagine this: You have a senior advisor with whom you work. She is showing signs of not being sharp anymore, and you are worried. You want to maintain the best ethics yourself, but you don't want to take on a problem of an impaired colleague by yourself. Here is a step-by-step protocol you might use. Yes, this is an ideal scene, and in a perfect world every organization would have this in place. In the real world, we need some steps to help us figure out if our colleague should step down from her duties. Here is how a protocol might work. This applies only to those in an organization of at least a few advisors and, possibly, a larger firm.

**Step One:** You observe the colleague you think is impaired. **You have a checklist available for assessing diminished capacity in your clients** that sets out the cognitive, behavioral and emotional signs of diminished capacity. You document **three instances** in which your colleague has demonstrated any of the red flags of diminished capacity. You note them as you would for a client, with the date of each observation and a description of why you are concerned. There is no set time period for your observations. Your documentation is completely confidential, and your name does not appear on it.

**Step Two:** After you document three separate instances of red flags of diminished capacity in your fellow advisor, you take the matter to your legal or compliance department, which has a **designated committee of aging-client experts** in place. The committee has expanded to also address age-impaired advisors. The committee reviews your documentation. It has a chair person who is tasked with approaching the impaired advisor. This committee can consist of a compliance officer, risk management person and management professional, or any combination of professionals tasked with addressing such issues in-house.

**Step Three:** The committee chair has a guideline script for what to say to the age-impaired advisor. She requests a **private and confidential meeting with the impaired advisor**. She starts with a statement that she is concerned. She indicates that others have observed a few instances which suggest that the advisor is having trouble keeping track of things, or has memory issues, or whatever was documented. She offers the advisor two options.

The first is to begin the process of succession of her book of business to another person voluntarily and to set a date for its completion. In other words, the apparently impaired colleague is urged to retire, if not required to do so. An end date is set.

The other is to obtain a confidential medical examination within a short, specified period of time. Some symptoms that appear to be cognitive problems may actually be from other causes.

Medication side effects, physical health changes, depression and other issues could be the source of the behavior others are seeing. If the advisor is medically cleared, and has no identified physical issues, he would be allowed to continue work under much closer scrutiny than before. If there is any recurrence of the observed signs of cognitive impairment originally documented by colleagues, the advisor would then be required to have an assessment of her capacity for managing financial matters from a licensed psychologist or neuropsychologist. If the assessment shows no impairment, the advisor is permitted to continue in the work as usual.

If the assessment shows impairment, which the advisor must disclose to the committee chair, the advisor is required to establish a date for retirement and a succession plan within six months of the date of the psychological assessment. During that six months, close supervision of the impaired advisor's actions would be in place.

All of these options would be spelled out in a company policy statement, along with all other employment-related documents or corporate statements of operation for the firm or office.

Perhaps this sounds like a fantasy solution to the issue of impaired colleagues in stages of obvious cognitive decline. Ideas about how to address it must start with using objective data as a guide, such as documentation you would create for any impaired client. That is not fantasy. It is real observed data. That would work where there are co-workers, colleagues and a setting that is created with more than one person in it.

And clearly with a solo advisor, there may be no one observing the age-impaired person at work. You may not see your own problem if you develop age-related decline of your mental functioning. For solos, be sure you have a friend to meet with regularly as you age, someone who can serve as a trusted colleague, who will tell you honestly if you seem to be getting into trouble.

What we suggest here is a **start** for any firm to create its own proactive protocols for the impaired advisor. We urge that some process be developed and put in place to address this problem of advisors who develop cognitive decline. It is inevitable that some will. And without any process in place, the firm or office is taking too great a risk of a dissatisfied client deciding that you are liable for financial losses permitted by an impaired advisor who should have stepped down long ago. We urge you to consider this and avoid potential liability. What you do for a living is complicated, and there is too much at stake to simply allow anyone who looks to you to be impaired to continue to manage clients' money. All can be exposed to client complaints or feel repercussions from age-related errors in a group setting. Without any control or effort to stop them when impairment becomes obvious, we think you will be exposed to consequences. As one of your authors is a former plaintiff's lawyer, we urge you to consider how your inaction might appear to a client's attorney hearing the client or family complaining about that advisor with dementia.

## Protecting Yourself: One Simple Thing Every Independent Advisor Should Do

As none of us can be assured that cognitive impairment won't affect US, we can at least keep a record of essential data, so that if we had a sudden event, accident or crisis in our lives, we would not leave those who would step in without anything to help them get started. The legal profession has anticipated the impaired or disabled lawyer who is in solo practice and has made recommendations. The American Bar Association produced the "Aging Lawyers Report" in 2007, from which I have borrowed an idea or two for this record of essential data. The appendix to the ABA report has a sample succession letter a lawyer could use to advise anyone taking over a solo lawyer's legal practice. Such a letter could be prepared and given to a friend or colleague for a financial advisor in independent practice as well. Since any of us can suffer an accident or other health issue, or die unexpectedly, it is helpful to designate a friend who could step in right away and deal with our business. If a person does develop dementia, a succession letter will help your colleague protect your book of business as someone else takes over your responsibilities. This sample letter could be used if an advisor dies suddenly, becomes ill or is unable to work for any reason. If you work alone, you can write this kind of letter and give it to that trusted friend you would want to help you or your family.

I have revised it to suit financial professionals, as follows.

**Sample Succession Letter**

[Full name of financial professional] [street and suite address] [city and state] [date]

Dear [fellow advisor full name]:

This is my letter confirming your agreement to step into the office in the event of my untimely death or disability. My errors and omissions coverage is with [name of professional liability carrier]. Policy number [policy number]. Their telephone number is [telephone number of carrier]. You have been identified to them as the person to manage my business in the event of sudden disability or death. That policy renewal date is [date of policy renewal].

My assistant is [full name of administrative assistant], his/her address is [full address and email] and telephone number is [telephone number].

A reliable colleague with a similar book of business to mine is [full name of colleague], address is [full address] and telephone numbers are [office and cell numbers].

The office accountant is [name of accountant] and his/her address is [accountant office and email addresses]. His telephone numbers are [accountant office and cell numbers].

My sign-in and passwords for the bank accounts I use are listed below [list all by name and account numbers].

Access to confidential client files and information is as follows [list username, passwords or other means of getting into information for every client].

[Name of executor] is the executor of my estate. That address is [street and email addresses of executor].

[Name of person with power of attorney] has a full power of attorney to act on my behalf, which includes signature power on all accounts.

[Name of insurance agent] is knowledgeable as to the office insurance policies which would come into play if you have to activate this letter. In addition to the general policies, there is a life insurance policy with [name of life insurance company], and that policy number is [number of life insurance policy]. That policy provides for a substantial amount of money to be paid to the corporation in order to permit the office to stay open until everything can be transferred or resolved. Its renewal date, in case of disability only, is [date of renewal for applicable insurance policy].

Client portfolio review schedule is on my computer marked [designate how you track], and to get into that file you need to [give sign-in and password].

The office checking account is with [name of bank with office account], account number [office checking account number]. Checks are located [designate], and PayPal or other payment-processing system is [name], and access is as follows [provide information that will allow your designee to process and deposit payments from any source].

Other online essential account information is [provide account names and purposes of account]. My online access is [sign-in and password].

Fee calculation information is contained in this program [name and provide access information].

The calendar program is [name of calendar program]. Anything that needs to be canceled is on that calendar.

For any independent maintaining a leased office:

My landlord is [name of landlord] and the lease expires on [date of lease expiration]. Other relevant information for all clients in your book should be enumerated somewhere so that a colleague can step in and address your clients' needs, protecting their investments and/or transferring responsibility to a new financial manager.

Sincerely, [your name]

Imagine yourself coming into the office of a disabled or deceased colleague and doing what needs to be done with his book of business. Include in your succession letter everything you would want yourself if you had to clean up and close down that office.

## SUMMARY

The issue of the age-impaired financial advisor is like an elephant in the room: No one is talking about it, but it's bigger than life and it's in our midst. With our aging population, people from every walk of life are developing dementia. None of us is immune from Alzheimer's disease or other forms of dementia. Some professions have a mandatory retirement age, as pilots do. But most everyone else can continue on with a license for as long as one wishes to do so.

In the descriptions of the architect, the trial lawyer and the financial advisor above, you could imagine how difficult it was for each of them to stop working. None of them was able to see their own impairments. In each of these true scenarios, colleagues were unable to address the problem. Sometimes it takes a disastrous event, or harm to a client, for colleagues to stop the impaired professional from continuing in the workplace. Sometimes, as with Mark, family was able to more or less pressure him into retiring. Sometimes a client complaint triggers a response to force retirement upon the professional through a licensing body or regulatory body.

We suggest that the issue of age-impaired colleagues be dealt with privately, first through the office where the professional is employed. If you have some basic protocols in place, and a path to follow for your approach, you have a chance of success. And, most assuredly, a private, confidential approach will not always work. Some cognitively impaired folks can be quite stubborn in refusing to acknowledge their problems. And it may not be their fault. Sometimes brain disease itself is the reason they cannot see their own impairments. Conscious denial may not be a factor.

If there is one thing you take from this chapter, let it be this: Impaired colleagues are inevitable. Be prepared, watch for the signs, and consider a thoughtful, kind approach to helping them, if you can, to give up the advisor role, even if that is gradually. Their financial safety, and that of their clients, will eventually be at stake, perhaps sooner than later.

# 8

# WRAP-UP: TAKE ACTION TODAY

**INTRODUCTION**

This is the last chapter, and it is basically your call to action. If you have read through all the other chapters, you have filled your head with a lot of ideas. Now we distill them into a few straightforward action steps anyone can take to be ready for what many are calling the "silver tsunami." That is a wave of aging clients in your practice now, or the one that is on its way to you. You will never be ready with a thoughtful approach unless you start immediately to shape a way to do business effectively with aging clients. These are different folks as age takes its toll. If your goal is to keep your clients for life, one must anticipate the effects of age just as you anticipate the effects of changes in the economy for all your clients. This chapter tells you how you personally can get a running start on putting to use what you have learned here in this book.

It makes no sense to learn a lot of new ideas, or reinforce the ones you had before with your oldest clients, and not do anything else but think about them. Here is where you decide how to actually make the first moves toward a senior-conscious, thoughtful strategy that makes you a better financial professional for senior clients. The checklist in Appendix 3 is a good jumping-off place, and we'll show you how to put it to use.

## Policy-Driven Preparation and Actions

Throughout this book we recommend development of senior-specific programs for advisors and their firms. We detail some essential components of such a program in Chapter 6. If you have a clear policy for seniors in place, you will know what to do when your client begins to demonstrate diminished capacity. You will have an appointed person to contact when you are concerned about those red flags you see in your client. You will not only have the contact information in your file for the person to call "just in case" there is a capacity issue with your client, but you will also have a document that gives you permission to make that call.

As no one can predict who will develop dementia or other cognitive problems and who will not, we have only the statistical likelihood to go on. Recall that the odds of developing Alzheimer's disease are at least one in three by the time your client reaches age 85. And remember, as well, that two-thirds of those diagnosed with Alzheimer's disease are women. Many older women are less knowledgeable about family finances than their male counterparts, so an unsophisticated female who is also developing dementia is at substantial risk for losing assets. As you think these things over, getting a senior-specific program in place may seem overwhelming. You're busy. Just keeping up with all the regulators' rules and staying compliant is a job in itself. The things we suggest and outline all take time from your busy day. How are you going to do even more? As with most complex tasks, break the job down into smaller pieces. Take it a little at a time.

## Approach the Senior Client Issue One Step at a Time

Here are some suggestions for a one-step-at-a-time approach to a workable program in your office.

You be the initiator, and think of a reasonable time frame to get this project off the ground. Where do you start? Figure out who the aging clients are first.

## 1. Database
How long would it take to create a database of clients in your book age 65 and up? If you have just one, it will be very easy! If you have more, it will simply take a review, perhaps by an assistant, if not by you, to find all clients by birth date and to make a list of them for your database. That is a fine first step, painless and essential to know how big a group you need to focus upon. Put it on your calendar to target an end date for getting your database done. Maybe this first piece can be finished by the end of this week.

## 2. The working group
If you work alone, and independent of any other organization, you can do most of this policy creation all by yourself. You will still need to run your ideas by someone, because there are legal items, like privacy, that require input from someone else. If you work with others, you need a working group, or your friends in the field, to help you create a new kind of plan for these seniors.

## 3. Meet regularly
You can set meetings for each month and tackle the program phases we outlined in Chapter 6 at each meeting. A mission statement takes little time to create. You know why you need to do this. It's to keep aging clients safer and to protect you and your firm. Write that down, and voilà! You have a mission statement.

## 4. Employ your checklists
We're making it easy for you to standardize how to get two of the most essential items together by giving you two ready-

made checklists (Appendix 1 and 2). If you want to keep aging clients safer as a general goal, you have to look at what makes them less safe as they age. Of course that includes diminished capacity and the risk of financial elder abuse. Now the task is to use a standardized way of checking for these risks and documenting them. Everyone in the organization should observe and document your senior clients' actions and risks in the same way, so you are all speaking the right language. Everyone needs the checklists. They may not cover every possible thing that can go awry with an older client, but they are a good start to standardize how you do things.

### 5. Aging-client portfolio reviews

Try out the checklists. If you review a portfolio with your older client, look for what's on the diminished capacity checklist. If the client seems perfectly okay, no worries for now, at least. If they're showing some of those warning signs of diminished capacity, you do need to act. This is where you and your colleagues decide how many warning signs will compel you to take further action. The same thing applies to warning signs of financial abuse. For that, you need a written policy statement that you will always report the problem you see.

### 6. Escalation

If you get bogged down figuring this out on your own, AgingInvestor.com can help. We have been immersed in studying these problems for the three years preceding the writing of this book, and we have heard from a lot of you about the stumbling blocks you face.

From your checklists you will need to decide on a uniform process for escalation of a client matter that worries you. A committee can be a first stop, though the committee needs to be better versed in aging issues than you are. From there, a problem can, and should, go to compliance, legal or risk management, according to how things work in your organization. If you are an independent, you will need help from the person(s) you would normally turn to with any legal question involving your clients.

## 7. Privacy

The privacy issue is a legal issue. It takes a legally sufficient document to get past the client's privacy rights. You will need legal input to get that part of your policy done. A document that addresses this and gives you the right to contact others is crucial. If you are stuck, and don't know how to make one, resources we offer at AgingInvestor.com will help you, including a ready-made product you can purchase that lays out an entire program with all the needed documents done for you. Otherwise, keep going and get that document done so that it is available to you for every aging client in your database. Such a document requires that you have your client name trusted third-party contacts you can call in when needed.

## Is This Urgent?

The urgency of creating a standardized way of managing aging clients depends on how many older clients you have. If you are a younger financial professional and your client base tends to be younger, you may not be feeling any pressure whatsoever. But if you have some clients in the 65+ age range, and increasing numbers of them are currently populating your book, now is the time to act.

One urgent matter for everyone to address is the financial elder abuse issue. The regulators are likely to require that you report elder abuse soon, as their model rules have already been publicly posted and commented upon. These may be the first of a series of new rules affecting financial advisors who are not bank-based. Banks now are mandated reporters in most places. How can you report financial abuse if you are not well aware of the warning signs? By the time you see the aftermath, the client's money is gone and not likely to be recovered. We prefer to focus on prevention. Prevention is not likely to become a rule, but the overarching concern of regulators is about keeping clients financially safer. That, to us, sounds like wanting you to use preventive strategies. Spot those warning signs using the checklist so you remember what to look for and what might be worth reporting.

**The Best Outcomes**
We see advisors struggling over what to do with a client who has diminished capacity. There seems to be a lack of rules about how to manage them everywhere we look. If you had a clear path to follow when you saw those red flags, wouldn't you feel more comfortable? Wouldn't it be great to have a place to go when you weren't sure how impaired your client was? Wouldn't it be a lot better to have some expertise on hand in-house so you could ask questions, kick it around with someone else in your organization or group, and then decide what to do?

We would like to see that outcome for you: that you would always have a place in your firm or group to take your questions about problematic older investors. And we would also like to see across-the-board policies that make it automatic that you have two or more third-party contacts in your file for every client, just in case. If you suspected a client was going downhill cognitively, you would document, discuss, decide and then bring in a third party to help you.

That third party would be familiar with your client's finances and ready to be the competent person taking your client's place in decision-making. This would be a systematic process protecting both you and the client.

Maybe we're dreaming here. But we do see this scenario of having a clear senior program as a possibility anywhere. Every part of it will take work and an investment of time. What a worthwhile investment! We are hoping that the early adopters among you will lead the way, because you don't want to lose clients, you don't want to lose fees and you genuinely care about your clients. Caring about clients is more than a slogan or marketing tool. Show it by protecting them as they age and perhaps become more vulnerable.

## Should You Wait for a Program Until Some Clients Are Diagnosed With Dementia?

As we have pointed out, a diagnosis of Alzheimer's disease or any dementia means that your client is already impaired. Why wait? It is impossible to know exactly where to draw the line with your older clients and when you must stop them from doing something financially dangerous because they have lost their capacity to make decisions. There is no magic buzzer that warns you "OKAY, now it's time! Get a program together!"

Every advisor needs to see every aging client as potentially in need of the protections that a senior-specific policy can afford them. Alzheimer's disease occurs over years, with gradual decline in most people. If a client begins to suffer memory problems in her 60s, and shows those red flags in her 70s, it does not matter whether she has had a formal diagnosis of Alzheimer's, or dementia, or not. Some people with dementia never do have an official diagnosis, but everyone around them realizes they are not okay. The point here is not to wait for a diagnosis from any doctor to tell you what you must do. And it is not at all proactive to wait until you have an impaired client to begin the process of developing a senior office policy. Leadership in your field, as in any field, requires anticipating problems and being proactive in solving them. You should have a clear direction when you see age-related problems in your clients. The program we are discussing gives you that clear path.

**The Bottom Line**
When your clients are being taken advantage of, you are losing money, as their funds are being drained out of the account you manage. It seems prudent, if for no other reason than not wanting to lose fees, that you would develop a greater interest in keeping senior investors financially safer than they are right now. And for those who have trusting and long-term relationships with clients who really rely on you, the incentive is even greater. You care about the client. You don't want to expose them to unnecessary danger because of their age-related vulnerability. You want to protect them and will spend the time it takes to do so.

Although many advisors have a basic familiarity with dementia, some from extensive personal experience, few have applied this familiarity to practical solutions at work. Knowing that some of your clients are impaired is not enough to solve the inherent problem you have when they do decline in capacity.

Regulators who are not in your shoes keep making rules you must follow. The legislature keeps piling on rules, too.

Sometimes it may seem that all you do is struggle to keep up with compliance. And we appreciate the burden you must feel. At the same time, we see a potentially explosive problem with the aging population that leaves you with no choice about addressing aging investors in a different way.

If you're smart about this, you are going to be ahead of the regulators. A firm-wide senior policy will help you know just what to do when you suspect financial abuse. When the regulators come along and make it mandatory that you report abuse, you will have nothing new to do. You'll already have a firm policy in place and will understand the process.

If a person in your own family suffered from dementia in any form, you may believe that you know what it's all about and that any client who has impairment will not be a problem. But your experience gives you a universe of one to draw from. Every senior client is different. Every person's manifestations of age-related issues is different. You need to be prepared for the client who is nothing like that parent or grandparent you helped at the last part of his life. The guidance we offer in this book is meant to be general enough that it can apply to just about anyone. And specific, different things will come up for you that we do not cover here. Stay curious. There is a best practice way to address every problem you will face.

As of this writing, the Department of Labor's fiduciary standard mandating that you do what is best for the client has become the rule for everyone in your industry. Everything we suggest in this book is directed toward the client's best interests and financial safety. We do not comment in any way about what products you should recommend, what senior designations you should use, or what marketing tactics you can use, or not, with older clients. Those are all outside the scope of our perspective as aging experts. What we do hope is that you will find at least some things here that you can do right now to step up the level of scrutiny over your older clients. And we hope you will keep at it until you become exemplary.

## The Measure of True Learning

What usually happens after you read a helpful book or article, take a continuing education course or attend a conference, is that you learn a few good things, think they make sense and intend to do something with them. Then you go back to your office with a thought in your mind about putting what you just learned into practice somehow. Work gets busy right away, or you have to act quickly on behalf of a client. Before you know it, the press of business takes your mind off whatever you learned and nothing new happens. It's back to the normal way of things. We've all done this, haven't we?

**It is said that true learning is manifested by a change in behavior.** And a change in your behavior is what we are aiming for here. It's fine to hear some good ideas. It's great if you like any of the concepts we've introduced in this book. But if nothing changes for you after reading it, it has not really taught you anything. The very best way to incorporate something is to use just one item, perhaps even one checklist, in your work with any client. That is how you use learning effectively. And it would be wonderful to see thousands of checklists in thousands of offices everywhere being used to assess the basic capabilities of your clients or to tell you when to step in where you suspect diminished capacity or possible elder abuse. What an uplifting change that would be!

## SUMMARY AND THE LAST WORD

In this chapter we have shown you a few simple steps to get you going on creating a special way to do business with your senior clients. It includes focusing on your own motivation to keep them safer, as well as your motivation to keep the clients and your fees. We gave you some basic suggestions that include creating a senior client database, working with colleagues, developing a statement of purpose and employing standard ways of identifying and documenting both signs of diminished capacity and signs of elder financial abuse. Privacy is an issue that can be dealt with if you are willing to take the time to use a privacy document to get your clients' permission to contact trusted third parties in case the need arises. These essential steps are major headway in developing the well-thought-out senior-specific office program you need.

The biggest takeaway we hope you glean from this is to do something! Telling yourself you'll get around to it when you have time will, of course, result in nothing getting done. Do at least one thing, and keep your commitment to yourself right now. Copy a checklist or two from this book and share it. Use it. When you do, you are truly demontrating that you have learned something about your senior clients.

It has been said that **the effect you have on other people is your best currency**. We encourage each person reading any of this to make that effect on your eldest, and perhaps most vulnerable, clients the thing that is stellar about you. Skill in financial management is one thing, and we presume that you already possess that. Skill in deftly managing seniors will set you apart, make you more valuable to anyone and, we hope, will make you proud of what you accomplish in demonstrating that skill.

## ABOUT THE AUTHORS

**Carolyn Rosenblatt, R.N.** and elder law attorney, has over 45 years of combined experience in her professions. She practiced nursing for 10 years and had a legal practice for 27 years before becoming an aging expert and consultant. She and her husband, geriatric psychologist Dr. Mikol Davis, founded AgingParents.com, a mediation and consulting service for families, and AgingInvestor.com, offering educational training and products for professionals facing aging issues. They focus on diminished capacity elder abuse, family conflicts and financial decision-making.

Ms. Rosenblatt has been quoted in the *New York Times, Wall Street Journal, Financial Planning, Next Avenue, AARP, Money, the National Safety Council Journal* and many other sources, as well as appearing on numerous radio shows answering questions about aging clients.

Ms. Rosenblatt blogs weekly at *Aging Parents*, on **Forbes.com.** She is published in national legal and nursing journals on the legal aspects of caregiving, mediating family conflict, elder abuse, diminished capacity and the health care issues of aging. She is a frequent speaker for organizations, care facilities and professional groups.

She is the author of **The Family Guide to Aging Parents: Answers to Your Legal, Financial and Healthcare Questions.** She also wrote **Working With Aging Clients: A Guide for Legal, Business and Financial Professionals,** published by the American Bar Association.

One of her essential missions is to prevent financial abuse of elders. She is at carolyn@aginginvestor.com. She and Dr. Davis have two grown children. They are located in San Rafael, California.

**Dr. Mikol Davis, clinical psychologist and gerontologist,** has over 44 years of experience as a mental health provider. He has served all age groups in general practice. In 2008, he began his focus on geriatric clients and co-founded AgingParents.com with his wife, Carolyn Rosenblatt. Together they help families resolve disputes related to aging loved ones.

Dr. Davis has expertise in diminished capacity for decision-making in aging adults. He provides evaluations for testamentary capacity, financial decision-making capacity and offers treatment for elders with anxiety, depression and other difficulties. He helps clients resolve intergenerational conflicts and communication issues.

He creates many online courses and products to assist professionals and the public with understanding aging issues. He volunteers as a settlement panelist for Marin County Courts in high-conflict family matters. He is an active Rotarian. Dr. Davis and Ms. Rosenblatt share a passion for elder abuse prevention.

As of this writing, they have been happily married for 33 years. Dr. Davis is at drmikol@aginginvestor.com.

## APPENDIX 1
### Checklist: 10 Warning Signs of Diminished Capacity

A report by the Securities and Exchange Commission's Office of Compliance Inspections and Examinations, North American Securities Administrators Association and Financial Industry Regulatory Authority outlined practices used by financial service firms for interacting with older investors. The report lists "signs," or "red flags," identified by firms that may indicate that an investor could have diminished capacity or a reduced ability to make decisions regarding their finances.

**These signs include, but are not limited to, a client who:**

☐ **1**-Appears unable to process simple concepts.

☐ **2**-Appears to have memory loss.

☐ **3**-Appears unable to recognize or appreciate the consequence of decisions.

☐ **4**-Makes decisions that are inconsistent with her current long-term goals and/or commitments.

☐ **5**-Demonstrates erratic behavior.

☐ **6**-Refuses to follow appropriate investment advice. This may be particularly concerning when the advice is consistent with previously stated investment objectives.

☐ **7**-Appears to be concerned or confused about missing funds in his/her account, where reviews indicate there were no unauthorized money movements or no money movements at all.

☐ **8**-Is not aware of, or does not understand, recently completed financial transactions.

☐ **9**-Appears to be disoriented with surroundings or social setting.

☐ **10**-Appears uncharacteristically unkempt or forgetful.

Seeing those red flags? Learn the next steps!
**Know What Actions to Take**
CONTACT US AT AGINGINVESTOR.COM, 844-315-4464

## APPENDIX 2
## Checklist: 7 Warning Signs of Financial Elder Abuse

**Knowing these warning signs** will help you take protective action for your clients. Look for:

- [ ] **1. Sudden or unexplained change of estate documents**

  Your client has always had a trusted person whom he appointed as an agent on his durable power of attorney forms some time ago. Suddenly, he changes and gives the DPOA power to a different person, and you question that new person's motives and behavior when that new person contacts you asking for information.

- [ ] **2. Client can't access her own funds**

  Your client, whom you've known for some time, is not able to access her own funds under your management and other financial assets and property. Her assets appear to be under the control of someone else, who has stopped your client from making any decisions about her money.

- [ ] **3. Unexplained, unexpected change of address**

  You receive a change of address notice indicating that your client is no longer receiving mail at the location where he has been for as long as you've known him. You heard nothing from him about moving and were sure he did not want to move. You question this change of address.

- [ ] **4. You can't reach your client**

  When you call your client, someone else answers the phone and says your client is out or otherwise unavailable. Your written communication attempts to contact your client receive no response. After many tries, you get the impression that someone is stopping your client from taking your calls. Your client is being isolated from you, and possibly others.

☐ **5. Odd change in investment behavior**
Your client has always been a conservative investor, preferring low-risk products over the long period of time you've known him. Suddenly, he wants to withdraw cash to put into things you consider highest risk, if not downright dangerous.

☐ **6. Unexplained large withdrawals**
In checking your client's account, you notice numerous large withdrawals, unexplained and completely outside the norm for your client. This uncharacteristic pattern is alarming.

☐ **7. A new "friend" or romantic interest suddenly appears**
Your client comes to your office with a relative or friend whom you have never met and who has never before been involved in your client's financial matters. Your client seems pressured to include this other individual in obtaining all of his account information and to direct transactions. Be suspicious.

The pervasive problem of Alzheimer's disease and other dementias can steal a client's financial judgment and make the person much more vulnerable to manipulation. Even if an elder is still competent, she may be subject to the improper persuasion, called "undue influence," of a family member or other trusted person.

What is financial abuse? The National Committee for the Prevention of Elder Abuse defines it as the illegal or improper use of an older person's funds, property or resources. It can take many forms. Seeing warning signs?

**Learn the next steps!**
CONTACT US AT AGINGINVESTOR.COM 844-315-4464

## APPENDIX 3
### Busy Advisors' Quick Start Senior Program Checklist

No time to get a whole program together? Okay, just do SOMETHING! Here are some action steps to take now to build the foundation of a senior program in your office of any size. These are a start. You can schedule getting the rest of your program together over time.

- ☐ **1.** Identify motivated leaders to start the process of program formation for your firm's/office's senior investors. Form a working group to undertake the project of policy development. You and one friend can be the leaders.
- ☐ **2.** State your purpose. Put it in writing.
- ☐ **3.** Create a database of all your clients age 65 and up, using birth dates. This is your senior population for your program.
- ☐ **4.** Copy and disseminate the Red Flags checklist so everyone with senior clients uses it at every portfolio review of these seniors. Use the same words to document that are on the checklist of warning signs.
- ☐ **5.** Copy and disseminate the 7 Warning Signs of Financial Elder Abuse checklist. Document with the same language as on the list, just as you do with the red flags of diminished capacity. Get the number of the nearest Adult Protective Services office, and keep it on your checklist so you can report suspicious activity.
- ☐ **6.** Go through every senior client file in your database and ask your client for at least two trusted others whom you could call in case of emergency or if your client was impaired. Keep that contact information in your client file.
- ☐ **7.** Schedule a review of every senior client at least twice a year. Schedule it quarterly if you already know that aging client is showing signs of cognitive impairment now.

## SUCCEED WITH SENIOR CLIENTS

This is a fine start for developing a great senior program, whether you are in a large organization or you're an independent working on your own.

**Learn the next steps in developing your office-wide senior progam.**
CONTACT US AT AGINGINVESTOR.COM, 844-315-4464

# APPENDIX 4
## Resources and helpful Internet links

**FTC New Program on Financial Scams Targeting Seniors**
http://www.consumer.ftc.gov/features/feature-0030-pass-it-on

**FINRA Securities Helpline for Seniors**
http://www.finra.org/investors/finra-securities-helpline-seniors?utm_source=MM&utm_medium=email&utm_campaign=NewsRelease_042015_FINAL

**Your Guide to Long-Term Care Planning**
http://blogs.mutualofomaha.com/express/files/2014/10/M28890_KiplingerMagInsert.pdf

**What You Need to Know About Long-Term Care Insurance**
http://www.lifehappens.org/wp-content/uploads/2013/10/Brochure-What-You-Need-to-Know-About-Long-Term-Care-Insurance.pdf

**Could Children Be Required to Pay for Their Parents' Long-Term Care?**
https://merrillconnect.iscorp.com/LTC/docservice/viewDocument?mcItemNbr=ICC12 TLC A TCII FRLMistakes to Avoid When Shopping for Long-Term Care Insurance

**Options for Covering Long-Term Care Costs**
http://www.kiplinger.com/printstory.php?pid=12171

**Updated Kiplinger LTC Workbook**
https://www.jhltc.com/uploadedFiles/LTC_Catalog/PDFs_for_Marketing_Materials/Education_Awareness/3533.pdf

**Don't Wait to Plan Long-Term Care**
https://www.jhltc.com/uploadedFiles/LTC_Catalog/PDFs_for_Marketing_Materials/Reprint_Articles/ltc_1446.pdf

# SUCCEED WITH SENIOR CLIENTS

**Four Quick Tips on LTC Planning**
https://www.jhltc.com/uploadedFiles/LTC_Catalog/PDFs_for_Marketing_Materials/Education_Awareness/ltc_1244.pdf

**Valuable Lessons on Long-Term Care Planning**
https://xs.moorewallace.com/customerfiles/GNWRII/edocs/LTC144573.pdf?a=-63211034

**The Most Asked Questions About LTC Planning: A 3-Step Guide to Smarter Long-Term Care Planning**
https://xs.moorewallace.com/customerfiles/GNWRII/edocs/LTC117044A.pdf?a=913065392

**Fresh Perspectives on LTC Planning**
https://www.jhltc.com/uploadedFiles/LTC_Catalog/PDFs_for_Marketing_Materials/Education_Awareness/ltc_1172.pdf

**National Center on Elder Abuse** http://www.ncea.aoa.gov

**United Way** http://www.211.org

**National Association of Professional Geriatric Care Managers**
http://www.caremanager.org

**Case Management Society of America** http://www.cmsa.org

**North American Securities Administrators Association**
http://www.nasaa.org

**Investor Protection Trust** http://www.investorprotection.org

**Eye on Elder and Special Needs Issues**
https://www.naela.org/Public/Library/Publications/Eye_on_Elder_and_Special_Needs_Issues/Public/About_NAELA/Media/Eye_On_Elder_and_Special_Needs_Issues.aspx?hkey=ec49563b-4b5e-49b7-b1e7-6add537dfc5b

**National Adult Protective Services Association**
http://www.napsa-now.org/get-informed/

**The Mini-Cog** http://geriatrics.uthscsa.edu/tools/MINICog.pdf

**Declining Financial Capacity in Mild Cognitive Impairment**
http://www.neurology.org/cgi/content/abstract/73/12/928

**Senior Investor Resource Center**
http://www.nasaa.org/1723/senior-investor-resource-center/

---

# RESOURCES FOR SENIORS

NASAA is working with AARP to ensure that senior investors are not being pressured into purchasing fraudulent or unsuitable investments at free lunch seminars.
**NASAA / AARP Free Lunch Seminar Monitor Program**
http://www.nasaa.org/1747/free-lunch-monitor/

Seniors should carefully check the credentials of individuals holding themselves out as "senior specialists."
**Misleading Senior Designations**
http://www.nasaa.org/1999/misleading-senior-designations/

Ten commonsense solutions to avoid investment fraud.
**10 Tips to Protect Your Nest Egg**
http://www.nasaa.org/1843/10-tips-to-protect-your-nest-egg/

A guide to having the money talk with your loved ones.
**Conversation Starters**
http://www.nasaa.org/investor-education/conversation-starters-empty-nest/

This NASAA-NAPSA-IPT program educates medical professionals and other caregivers about how to identify seniors who may be vulnerable to financial abuse.

## SUCCEED WITH SENIOR CLIENTS

**Elder Investment Fraud and Financial Exploitation (EIFFE) Prevention Program** http://www.nasaa.org/1733/eiffe/

Senior Summits allow state securities regulators the opportunity to come together with the SEC and FINRA to coordinate joint enforcement and education efforts to protect senior investors from investment fraud.

**Seniors Summit** http://www.nasaa.org/1966/senior-summit/

A quick reference checklist to help investors ask the right questions before making an investment.

**INVESTIGATE Before You Invest**
http://www.nasaa.org/wp-content/uploads/2011/08/Investigate-Checklist.pdf

**Senior Investor News & Alerts** http://www.nasaa.org/category/investor-education/seniors/senior-news-alerts/

**Top 10 Investor Traps**
http://www.nasaa.org/3752/top-investor-traps/

Take our 12-question quiz and learn what you can do to avoid becoming a victim of investment fraud.

**Investment Fraud Awareness Quiz** http://www.nasaa.org/3246/investment-fraud-quiz/

A variety of investor education publications and brochures.

**Investor Education Library**
http://www.nasaa.org/2420/investor-education-library/

NASAA members and other consumer education organizations offer excellent resources to help seniors better understand their investments.

## Additional Resources for Seniors
http://www.nasaa.org/2051/additional-resources-for-seniors/

## Get Help from Your State or Provincial Securities Regulator
http://www.nasaa.org/about-us/contact-us/contact-your-regulator/

## AgingInvestor.com

### AgingInvestor.com Social Media Channels

https://www.youtube.com/AgingInvestor
https://twitter.com/AgingInvestor
https://www.facebook.com/aginginvestor
http://www.forbes.com/sites/carolynrosenblatt/
https://www.linkedin.com/in/drmikol
https://www.linkedin.com/in/carolynrosenblatt

Made in the USA
San Bernardino, CA
25 May 2016